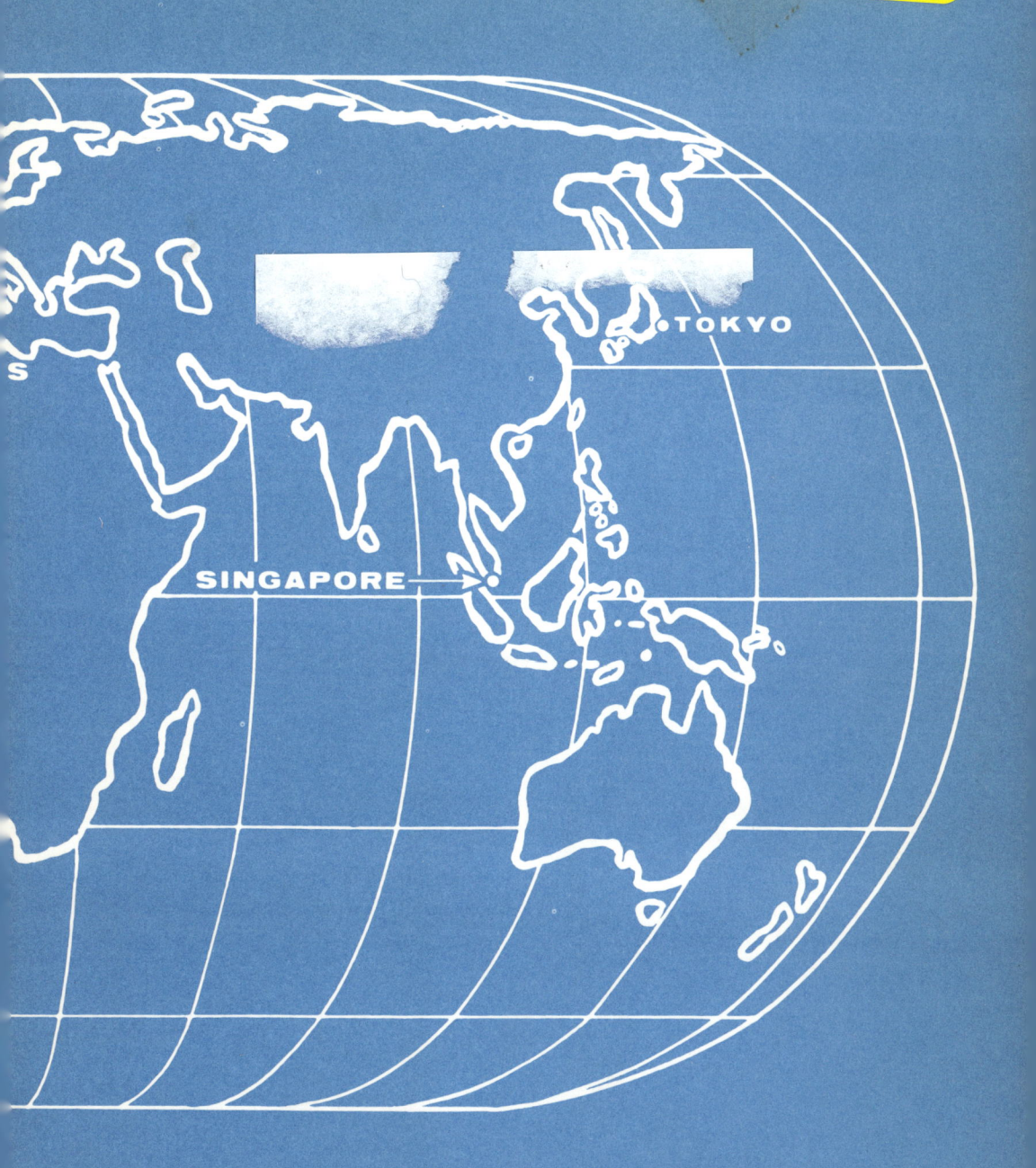

SINGAPORE

TOKYO

*Living
in
Singapore*

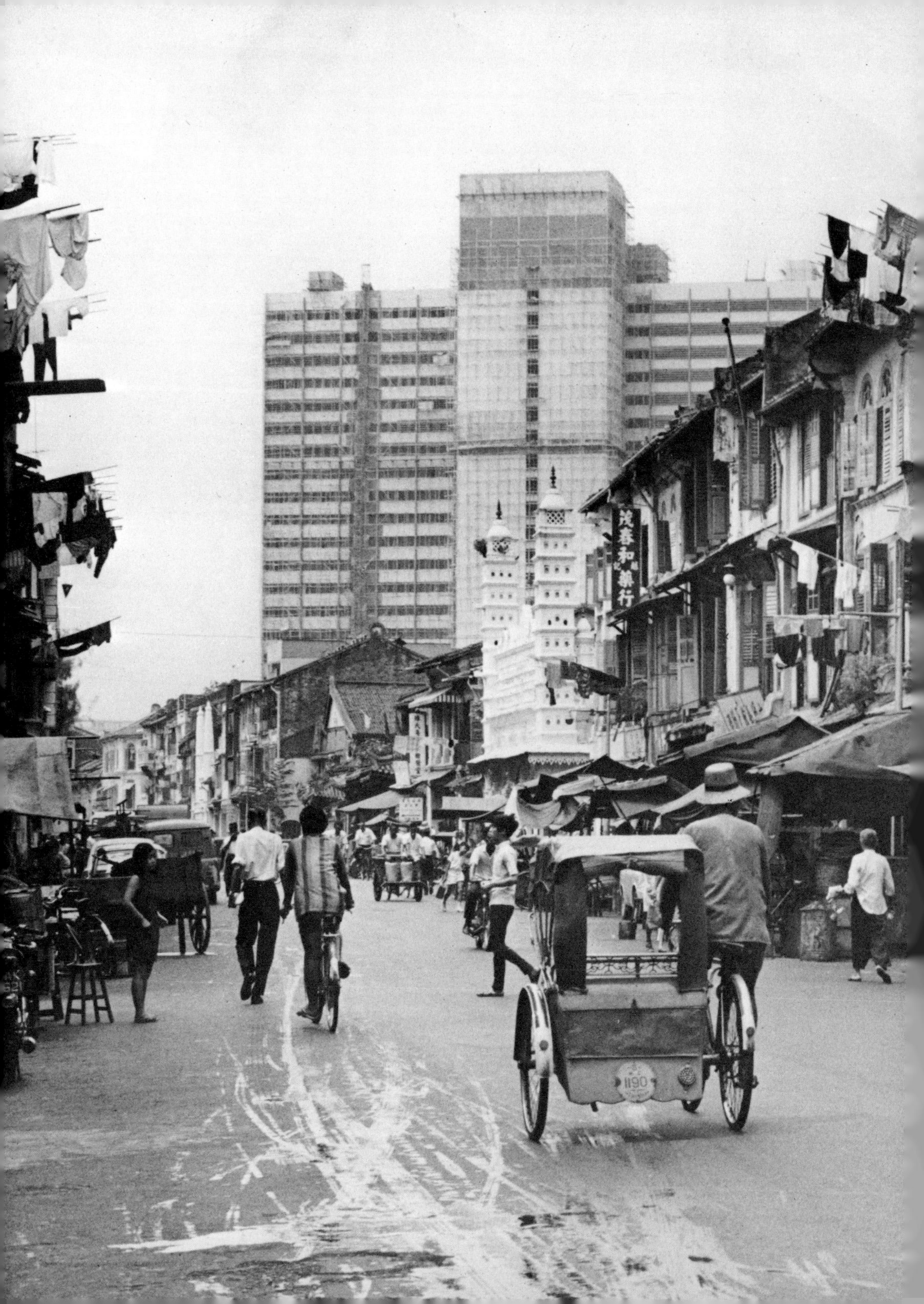
茂春和藥行
1190

Living in Singapore

Gwenn R. Boardman

THOMAS NELSON INC.
New York   Camden

All photographs are by Gwenn R. Boardman with the exception of the following from Port of Singapore Authority, p. 85; Shell Oil Company, p. 92; and Singapore Ministry of Culture, pp. 8, 102, 112, 121, 123. Permission is gratefully acknowledged.

© 1971 by Gwenn R. Boardman

All rights reserved under International and Pan-American Conventions. Published in Camden, New Jersey, by Thomas Nelson Inc. and simultaneously in Don Mills, Ontario, by Thomas Nelson & Sons (Canada) Limited.

Library of Congress Catalog Card Number: 74-140079

International Standard Book Number: 0-8407-7130-4
0-8407-7131-2 NLB

Printed in the United States of America

Contents

    Map   7
1. City of the Lion   9
2. At Home in the City   19
3. Chinese Families   31
4. The Malay Heritage   45
5. Indian Families   57
6. Schools for Everyone   71
7. The Port and Industry   83
8. At Play in Singapore   99
9. Festivals and Celebrations   113
    Index   126

Children climb on stage for a closer view of the *wayang* performers, who reenact stories of princesses, emperors, and magic on open-air stages

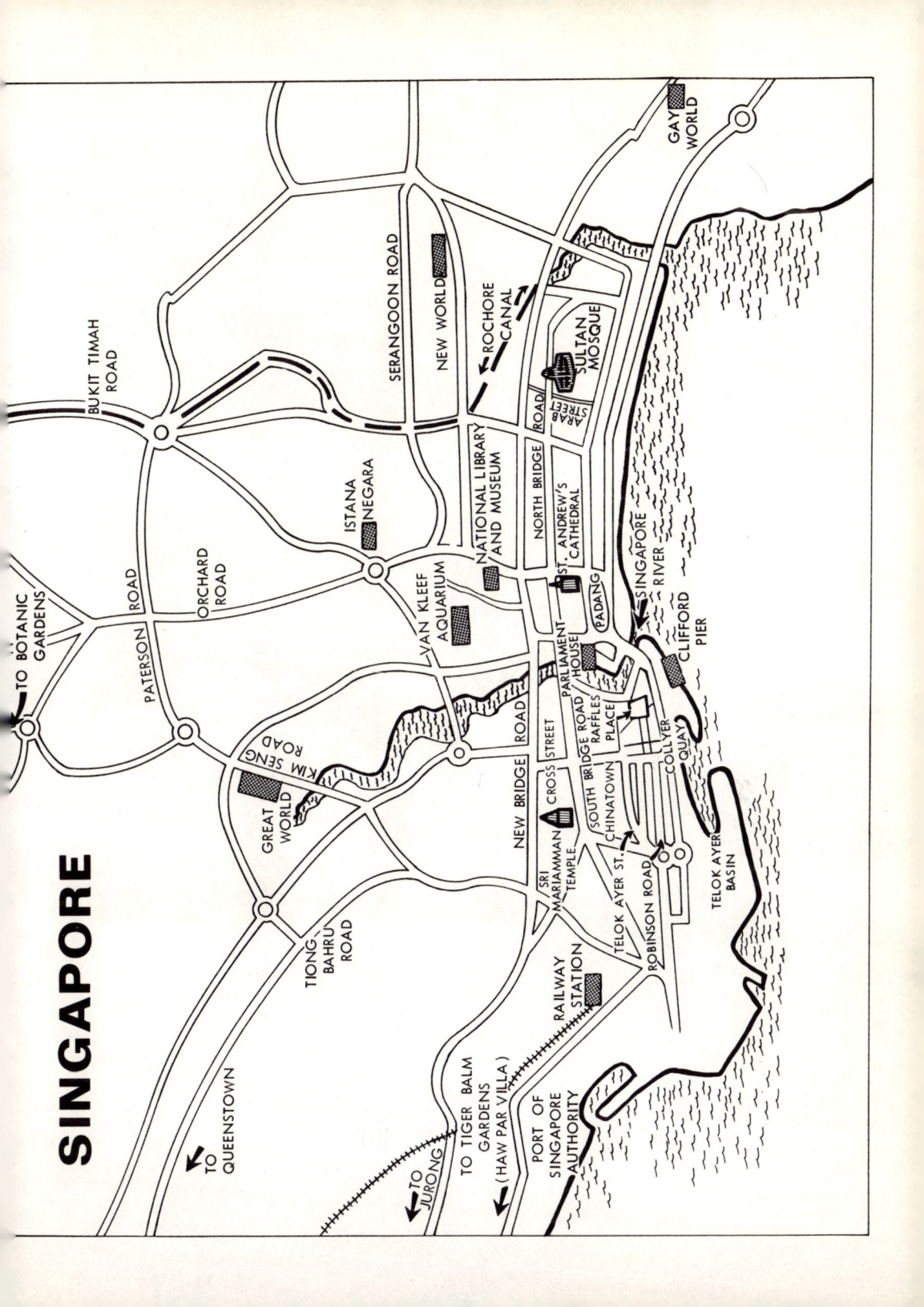

SINGAPORE

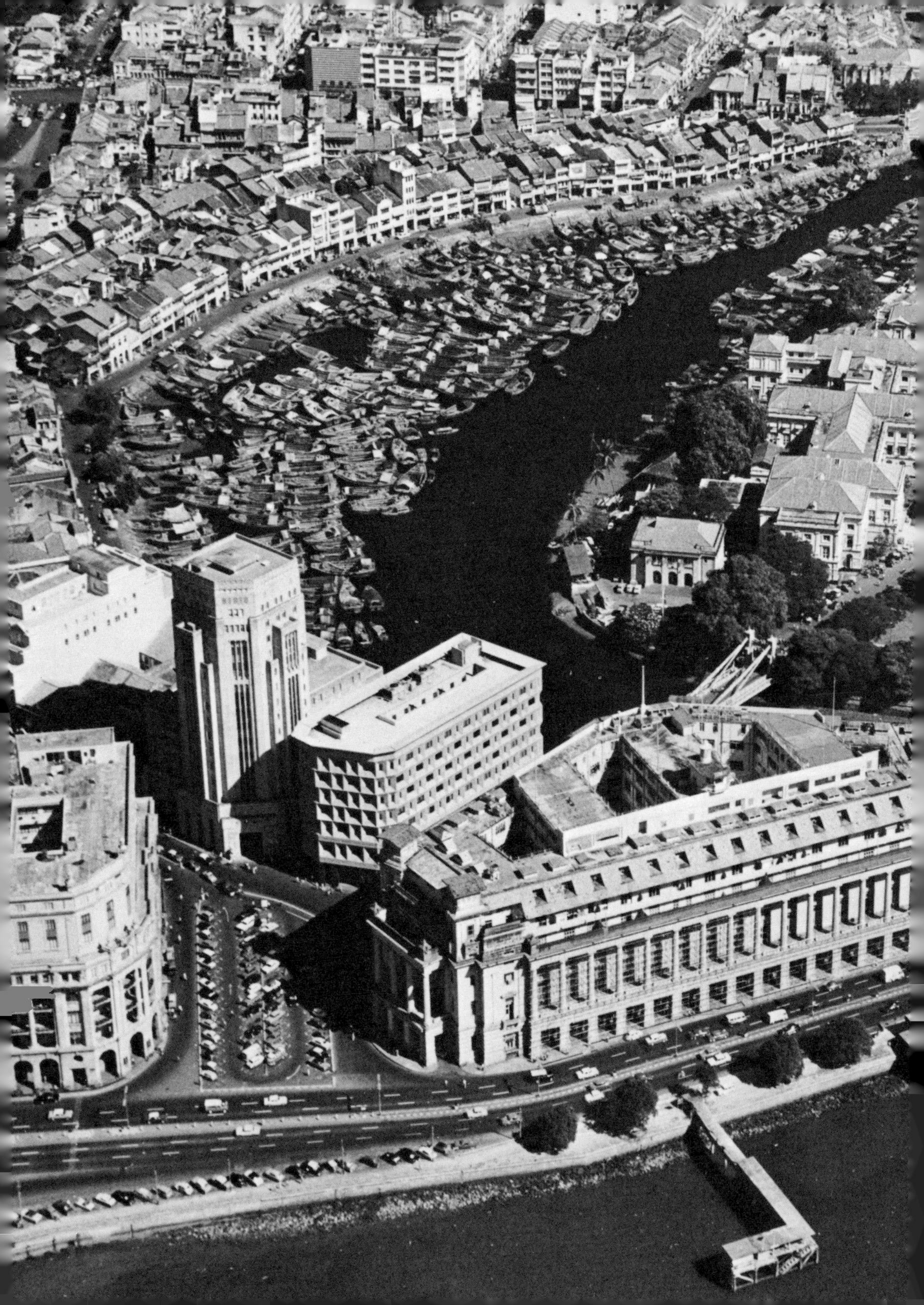

1. City of the Lion

SAIL through the Dragon Teeth Gate to the Lion City. You are in Singapore—a state, a republic, an island, a port, and the youngest city in Asia. More than half the people are under twenty years old. But whatever their age, they all seem to be out on the busy streets of Singapore at once.

Towering glass-and-concrete offices look down on men wearing Sikh turbans, on women in Indonesian and Malay sarongs, and on boys wearing the Malay *songkok* (cap). Chinese girls in *cheongsam* or in *samfoo* walk beside others in the latest London fashions. Everywhere there are sounds: pop tunes from New York, the clash of Chinese cymbals, and the beat of Malay drums. You hear half a

The Singapore River, filled with many small cargo boats, flows past hundred-year-old godowns, or warehouses, and several public buildings

Singaporeans board the Kuala Lumpur express. One Chinese woman appears in modern dress, a Malay woman in *baju kurong*, another Chinese woman in the Malay *sarong kebaya*, and a third in the traditional *samfoo*.

dozen Chinese dialects as well as Malay, Tamil, Arabic, and Hebrew. You also hear the accents of Oxford, London, and Sydney. The babel reminds you of the variety of cultures and the many nationalities that have contributed to the growth of this island of 225 square miles.

As you walk along, you recognize the signs of this heritage. Three out of four Singaporeans have Chinese ancestors, so you are not surprised by the number of shop signs written in beautiful Chinese ideograms (picture-words). Many merchants came originally from southern India or northern Ceylon, and their shop signs in the Tamil script advertise everything from bangles to saris and snuff. Nearby are Malay banks and shops, some with signs in *rumi* (romanized script), others in *jawi*, the adapted Arabic script written from right to left. One bank has its name written in Chinese ideograms, in English, and in *jawi*.

CITY OF THE LION

Even the street signs are multilingual. In public places, in parks, and outside the Immigration Office and the Registry of Births and Deaths, you see signs written in all four of Singapore's official languages: Malay, English, Chinese, and Tamil. The national language is Malay, and the language of administration is English.

That is not surprising, since today's modern and busy city grew out of a trading post established by an Englishman, Sir Stamford Raffles. This son of an English ship's captain went to work for the East India Company when he was fifteen years old. He was posted to Penang, became interested in Malay language and culture, and by the time he was thirty was appointed Lieutenant Governor of Java. On January 29, 1819, Raffles landed on the island of Singapore. He bargained with the Sultan of Johore for trading rights, and five years later the British purchased Singapore Island.

When Raffles first saw Singapore, only a few farmers, plantation owners, and fishermen lived there. There was no city, although Raffles later wrote that the area was "the navel of the Malay countries." He realized that it would make an excellent site for a port, lying between the China Sea and the Indian Ocean. Tin and rubber from the Malay Peninsula and rich spices and minerals from the islands of Indonesia also began to flow through Singapore to European and American ports before the century ended.

LIVING IN SINGAPORE

Today, exotic raw materials from all over Southeast Asia continue to be shipped through the port of Singapore. You can smell the spices that sent Columbus looking for new routes to the rich Indies. Cloves, coffee, sandalwood, pepper are all around you. Elephant tusks, gold dust, and gambier are ready for shipment too. Pigs (bars) of tin are lifted aboard ships, while great balls of Malay rubber bounce on the dock.

The modern port dates from the nineteenth century, yet Chinese chronicles of long ago tell of Temasek, meaning "Sea Town." This city probably stood where Singapore is now, and Chinese mariners knew the entrance to Singapore as Dragon Teeth Gate. Today's wide western entrance to Keppel Harbor was then only a narrow passage between two hills shaped like the cable pegs ("dragon teeth") of Chinese junks.

Ancient Malay Annals tell of a prince of Sumatra who gave the city its present name. Sang Nila Utama came to the island during a storm. Then he saw a strange beast, swift and beautiful, with a bright-red body. Its head was jet black, and its breast was white. Its size was "rather larger than a he-goat," but the people said it was a lion! According to the Annals, Sang Nila Utama answered: "If this is the way the animals look, it would be a good place to found a kingdom." So he called it *Singa-pura*, "Lion City."

CITY OF THE LION

That city was destroyed by the Majapahit Empire of Java in the 1370's. Later it became a small trading community, with a prince in charge of the port, but warfare closed the city once again in the seventeenth century.

The opening of the Suez Canal in 1869 launched a new era of prosperity for Singapore. In the twentieth century the demand for tin and rubber helped make this city one of the world's leading ports. Some goods are still transported in junks and *tongkangs* (small cargo boats) like the vessels of long-ago seamen. But there are also great ships bringing manufactured goods from all over the world to exchange for the raw materials of Southeast Asia—200,000-ton tankers bring oil to Singapore's refineries, and container ships load the products of Singapore's own new industries.

The modern buildings of Singapore's international trade rise up to fifty stories above the old godowns (warehouses), shops, and homes built a century ago. A modern car park overlooks streets where children still ride to school and housewives to market in trishaws. International businesses crowd Collyer Quay, overlooking the harbor, and line Robinson Road and Raffles Place. The Chinese refer to Raffles Place as European Firms Street, although it actually houses firms from all over the world, including some American companies, whose employees help to make up the four hundred American families in Singapore today.

LIVING IN SINGAPORE

Past and present, Europe and Asia blend on these streets. You glimpse the life of ancient China in the narrow street of the coffin makers. Yet a few blocks away a modern fire engine arrives at a construction site, where another tall building will soon tower above the old bazaars. Department stores and Indian bazaars stand side by side, while an itinerant Chinese peddler pauses in front of a modern supermarket. Gold bangles glitter in the showcase of a Chinese goldsmith. Nearby, gem cutters from Ceylon show a fortune in star sapphires, rubies, and diamonds. At the world's biggest bargain basement, Singapore's *pasar malam*, the night bazaar set up at a different location each

This decorative gateway, typical of South Indian temple architecture, leads to Sri Mariamman, the oldest Hindu temple in Singapore

evening, you buy batik fabric from Java, toys from Japan, and records cut in London.

You can find synagogues in Singapore, or worship at one of the island's hundreds of temples, mosques, and churches. These range from an Armenian church and Buddhist temples to Taoist altars and a Roman Catholic church founded by the Portuguese Mission. You can even catch a glimpse of the English countryside, the spire of St. Andrew's Cathedral, as you stand on the grass beneath shady trees. Listening to the early service at this hundred-year-old Anglican church, however, you discover that the words sung to the familiar tunes are Mandarin (Chinese). Later, as parishioners arrive for the English service and choirboys and girls gather, you see an Indian and his Chinese friend arm in arm, while a group of English and Indian mothers exchange greetings.

Although this island is set at the tip of the Malay Peninsula, joined to the mainland by a three-quarter-mile causeway, its Malay population makes up only 14 percent of more than two million citizens, while 74 percent are Chinese and 8 percent Indian or Pakistani. About three fourths of the Republic's population lives in the thirty-seven square miles of the city of Singapore. The entire island, however, is only twenty-six miles from east to west at its widest point and fourteen miles north to south. Even the many small islands of the Republic all lie within six miles

LIVING IN SINGAPORE

of the central city, and so everyone in Singapore knows the far villages and beaches as well as the bazaars, the markets, and the great government buildings of downtown Singapore.

Here stands one of the world's youngest Parliaments: its first Prime Minister (Lee Kuan Yew) was elected in 1959. A member may speak in any one of the four official languages, while his colleagues listen to simultaneous translations.

Singapore has been an independent republic only since 1965. After the island had been ceded to the East India Company in 1824, it eventually became one of the British Straits Settlements—then a Crown Colony in 1946 and a state in 1958. Singapore became self-governing in 1959 and joined the newly formed Federation of Malaysia in 1963. On August 9, 1965, Singapore withdrew from the Federation and became a sovereign republic within the British Commonwealth. On December 22, 1965, Inche Yusof bin Ishak was installed as first President of the Republic.

This modern republic has none of the usual disadvantages of the tropics. Even tropical diseases have been all but eliminated, and this was one of the first areas in the world to establish malaria control. Antimosquito campaigns keep the islanders healthy today. Should they fall sick, there are hospitals with internationally trained staffs

CITY OF THE LION

and such modern equipment as an artificial-kidney unit. Most services in the eleven government hospitals are free.

Modern hygiene is not confined to gleaming hospitals, though. The sidewalk barber's customers perch on newly painted stools before a tiny mirror, while he uses gleaming shears. Even the roadside eating stalls are as clean as home dining rooms. At any time of the day or night, Singapore's families, office workers, and shopkeepers are enjoying the most famous local dish: *satay*. Meat is marinated in sugar, salt, and spices before being grilled on a stick. The cook fans the charcoal beneath the skewered meat, quickly passing sticks to waiting customers. Jars filled with relishes line the counter, and you dip the *satay* into a sauce made with ground peanuts, coconut milk, and spices. It costs only ten Singapore cents to buy a stick of *satay*. Three Singapore dollars equal one American dollar, but for your ten Singapore cents you also get side dishes of rice, cucumbers, and onions. Enjoying lunch, you can watch the multiracial citizens of Singapore go by.

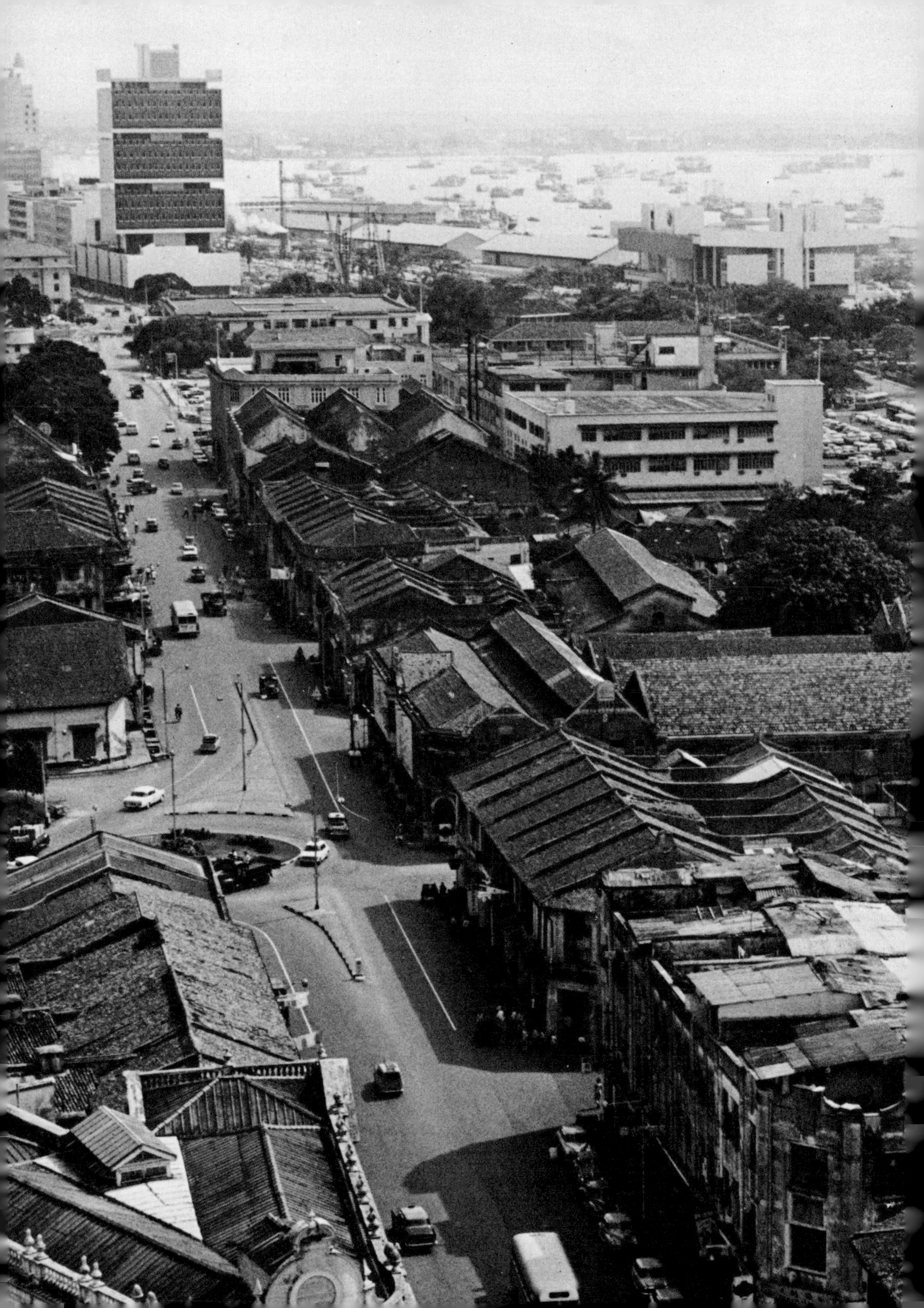

2. At Home in the City

HOME in Singapore may be a shop-house in Chinatown or a luxury apartment in Tanglin. It may even be an *attap*-roofed house in a *kampong* (Malay village). The daily bread may be Indian *chapatties*, breakfast may be a bowl of Chinese pork soup, and dinner may be a Malay rice dish, *nasi lemak*. The housewife may be wearing a sari, a sarong, or *samfoo*. You can visit homes in which customs, language, and even clothes are those of remote Chinese villages, Indian cities, or Malay jungles. But you will also find that many families live much as they would in Liverpool or in Philadelphia.

In central Singapore, modern highrises overlook the shophouses of an older era which are soon to disappear with urban renewal

LIVING IN SINGAPORE

Whatever their minor differences, one third of all the people in Singapore today live in modern apartments of the new housing estates. Since 1960 the Housing and Development Board has been busily changing the face of Singapore with blocks of apartments that rise as high as sixteen stories above the ground. These blocks are clustered in "estates" or "new towns," in which more than half a million people from crowded city apartments have already been rehoused. At the peak period, the board built one residential unit every forty-five minutes, a complete ten-story block of 120 units every four days!

Queenstown is home for 110,000 people, and as the first of Singapore's "new towns," it is the best place to see how the average family lives. It really is a town, too, for everything necessary for day-to-day life can be found right in the Queenstown Estate. Schools provide for all the languages of Singapore's citizens. Shops sell clothing, food, furniture, and oil. You can worship at a Chinese temple, a Roman Catholic or a Protestant church, or a mosque. There are clinics, fire stations, and all the services to take care of families. Entertainment is provided right in the neighborhood as well, and occasionally the circus comes to town. There are even jobs in nearby light industries, although most of the men commute to central-city employment.

Queenstown Estate has its own schools, playing fields, shops, and places of worship

Similar apartment blocks can be found in the older areas of Singapore, some overlooking the traditional markets near Rochore Canal or the bazaars of Arab Street. Laborers who work in the brick factory or the power station live in blocks at Pasir Panjang. The Port of Singapore Authority provides flats for its workers within walking distance of the port. Other estates are going up in the areas of Singapore's new industries. Flats at the Jurong Industrial Complex at the western side of the island are being filled by city workers who have moved out of overcrowded slums to take jobs in Jurong's new multistoried factories, shipyard, flour mill, and docks.

Many of Singapore's more expensive homes look much like suburban London houses, while others are "California garden bungalows" with five bedrooms. Inside, they are often little different from the flats in the housing estates, although there will perhaps be parquet or mosaic flooring instead of cement or linoleum. Rooms in the luxury housing will be larger, and there will be a servant's room or even separate quarters for the staff frequently employed in well-to-do Asian homes. Basically, though, all these homes are designed for Singapore's tropical climate.

Sitting on the veranda of a European-style house, you enjoy the cool shade of a wide overhanging roof. Such roofs and the large verandas encircling older houses are protection against tropical sun as well as the heavy rains of the monsoon. Air conditioning is a luxury, but many homes have slowly revolving electric fans overhead. They also have quite a few *chichaks* on the ceiling. These are the house lizards of Singapore, and they are guaranteed to keep insect pests under control. Outside your window, orioles sing, and insects chirp among the tropical foliage. In the towering apartment blocks, the garden may be replaced by potted plants on the balcony, while the gay song

Plants flourish in a Queenstown balcony garden

of birds comes from half a dozen cages hanging overhead.
 One of these balcony gardens is outside the apartment of a typical family in Queenstown. There are three boys and a girl between the ages of nine and fourteen, all sharing one bedroom. Their bunk beds are curtained off, rather like sleeping compartments on a train, while the opposite wall is lined with drawers and counter space. The living room

A Chinese housewife prepares dinner in her tiny Queenstown kitchen

does double duty as dining area, father's studio (he is an artist), and children's after-school study, as well as providing space for the refrigerator that will not fit into the small kitchen. In this kitchen, there are two gas burners, although other apartment tenants have purchased English-style gas-cookers (with ovens), use electric rice-cookers, or make the familiar *satay* over a charcoal grill. Above the cooking shelf there is storage space for traditional Chinese

AT HOME IN THE CITY

porcelain soup spoons and bowls alongside such modern conveniences as instant coffee and meat tenderizer.

   This housewife has probably done all her shopping at the estate's stores. At Singapore's up-to-date supermarkets, though, you can imagine yourself in any of the big cities of the world. Of course there are reminders that you are in Asia. The delicatessen sells curry puffs alongside German

At the local marketplace, a fish vendor weighs her wares on the *daching,* a hand-held scale

LIVING IN SINGAPORE

sausage, and the housewife bending over the frozen food locker is wearing a sari. One whole section is reserved for Chinese delicacies, and the labels of familiar soap powders are printed in Chinese characters as well as in English.

Frozen foods and groceries imported from the United States or from Europe, however, are found in few homes. Most housewives prefer to bargain for chickens (plucked live from big baskets), fresh fish, fruits, and vegetables in the markets of Singapore's Chinese and Indian areas. The marketplace is a center of multiracial exchange for Singapore families. Two Sikhs carrying shopping baskets buy their week's groceries. A shaven-headed Buddhist buys a pot of orchids from a small Chinese boy. A Chinese woman bargains for local fish by their Malay names, *merah* (red snapper) and *kerapu* (grouper). Others select dried squid or tiny shrimp. Bargaining is a favorite Southeast Asian activity, and no one expects to pay the asking price.

At home, the housewife will get out her *kwali*, a Chinese pan with a curved bottom, for cooking vegetables. Indian kitchens in the modern flats still include a flat cast-iron pan for making *chapatties* (thin sheets of bread) and an array of heavy earthenware pots. The Indian housewife prepares curry with the aid of a grinding stone. She rolls the long "pin" over a stone slab as she prepares chilies to mix with coriander, coconut milk, and saffron. Her Malay neighbor

At an outdoor eating stall, the proprietor cooks *satay*, a local delicacy of spicy, marinated meat

uses a pounding stone to crush chilies for *sambal*, one of the varieties of prawn paste served as a side dish with curry.

A kitchen that includes a stone rolling pin may also have an electric mixer, and occasionally you will find the housewife reaching into her refrigerator for one of the supermarket's frozen desserts. A charcoal pot for *satay* may stand beside an electric oven, although Chinese and Malay recipes do not include baked foods. Singapore is full of such surprises, and you may find that you are offered a bowl of noodles or of Chinese rice porridge for breakfast instead of cereal and milk. Many families do not follow the Western three-meals-a-day pattern, in which some foods are reserved for a particular time of day. But quite a few would

LIVING IN SINGAPORE

offer you toast and coffee in the morning, since many local children enjoy sweet coffee, well diluted with milk.

Whatever the favorite foods of these Singapore families, you can be sure that breakfast will be early. Students attend morning and afternoon sessions in alternate years, and morning classes begin at 7:45. Dressing for school always means putting on a smart uniform, whether they attend a government or a private school. Boys wear white shirts and

Automobiles, buses, and motorcycles whiz past the muscle-propelled trishaw

AT HOME IN THE CITY

starched shorts like those worn in English schools. Girls wear white blouses and colored skirts or gym tunics. Students living in Queenstown can see their school from the apartment windows, so there is no excuse for being late. But there are no school buses. Children living in the inner city join the crowds of commuters on city buses or enjoy the local equivalent of taxis and buses, the trishaw.

Morning classes end by 12:45, but many students pause at the school tuck shop (or canteen) for a hot lunch costing as little as twenty Singapore cents. Home again in his Queenstown flat, a typical Chinese boy then settles down to his English homework, just as his Malay and Indian neighbors are doing. The food on his dinner table, the clothes he wears, and the bed he sleeps in are all similar to those of his neighbors, too. Yet you can go to another section of Singapore and see Chinese boys and girls living in a world that seems far away from the modern city. That section is Chinatown. . . .

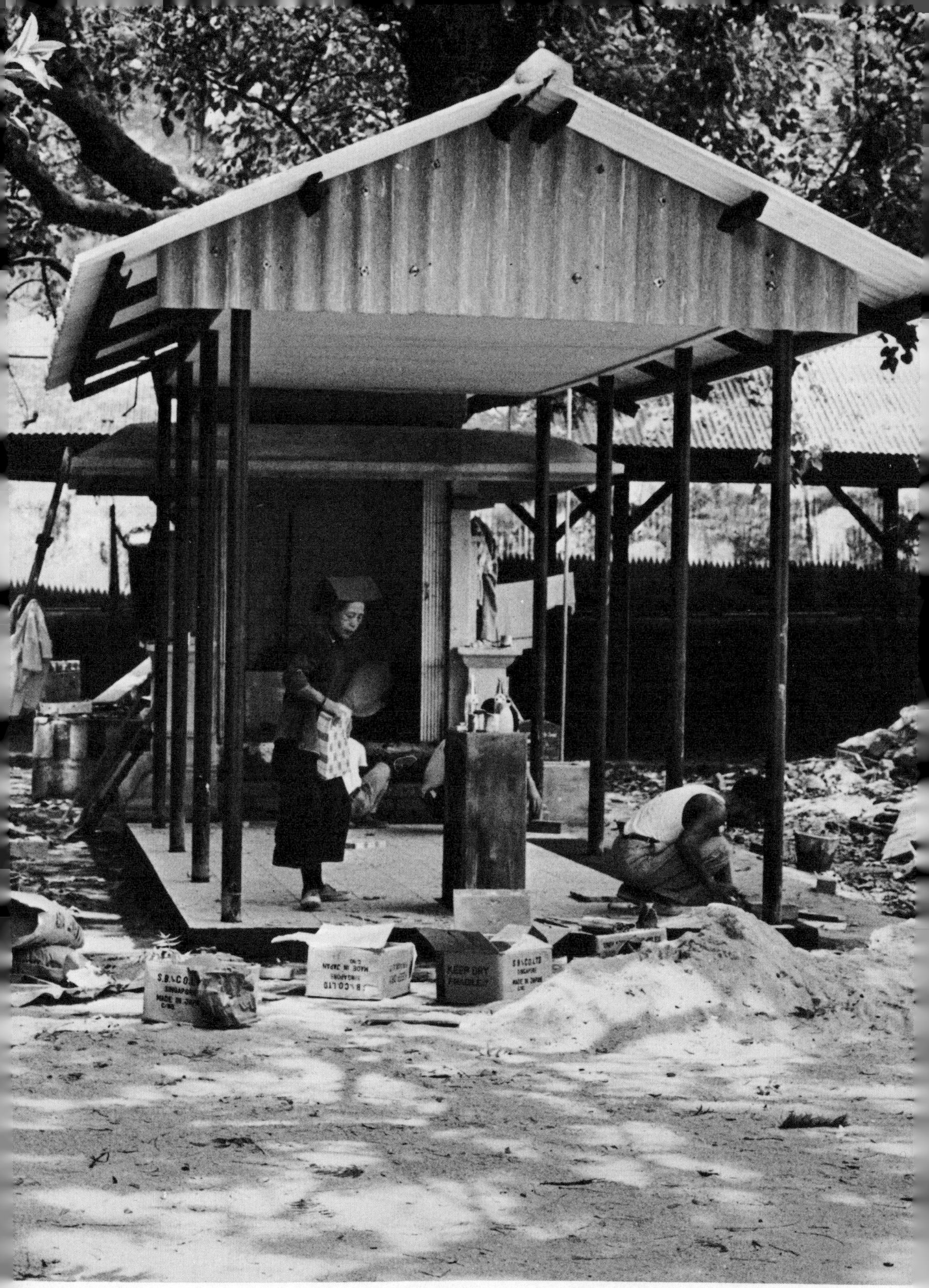

3. Chinese Families

TINKER, tailor, soldier, sailor... The old rhyme might well apply to the range of Chinese men and women who helped to found and develop modern Singapore. Three fourths of the citizens of today's city are of Chinese descent. But more than 60 percent of these Chinese citizens are natives of Singapore, many of them fourth- and fifth-generation descendants of workers who helped change the almost deserted island into today's bustling city-republic. And like American descendants of *Mayflower* voyagers or European immigrants, they look not to the past but to their present allegiance, saying, "I am not Chinese. I am a Singaporean."

Of course all Chinese residents are not confined within

This Sam Sui woman, a construction worker by trade, is helping erect a Hindu temple

the narrow area known as Chinatown. In multiracial Singapore, you are just as likely to find a Chinese worker carrying her baskets past the mosque where a group of Malay Moslems worship or even helping to lay the new foundation for a Hindu temple. Nor are all of them confined within particular occupational or social groups. They range from the modern leader, Prime Minister Lee Kuan Yew, to office workers and uniformed schoolgirls. There are wealthy businessmen whose luxury apartment rental is higher than a laborer's annual wage, and families who live in tiny cubicles not much larger than a king-sized bed. There are scientists, teachers, and engineers. Some men and women still practice the crafts of their ancestors, while others follow regional occupations. The Hakka, for instance, are in agriculture, and the Sam Sui women are highly valued construction workers.

Singapore was known to Chinese historians long before these immigrants journeyed to the new country. About A.D. 231, Sun Chuan, Emperor of Wu, sent envoys to Southeast Asia. They wrote home about an "island at the end of a peninsula." Chinese historians told of Temasek being attacked by the Siamese in the middle of the fourteenth century. When Sir Stamford Raffles arrived, about twenty gambier plantations were already in the area. Their Chinese owners were present at the ceremonies held for

CHINESE FAMILIES

the signing of the treaty between the Sultan of Johore and the East India Company in 1819.

In the following century and a half, thousands of Chinese workers came to Singapore. Among the earliest were laborers and craftsmen who came alone, leaving their families in China. Some of these laborers had been sold, for under twenty dollars, to Malay mine owners and to Chinese businessmen and farmers. In exchange for their passage and one year's work, these indentured laborers were freed. Some eventually saved enough money to lease tin mines from the Malay owners or to set up small busi-

A carpenter at work

nesses. Many adopted the customs and even the language of their Malay neighbors.

Today, you will find the *peranakan*, "born in the country," enjoy Malay *satay* with a Chinese flavor, using pork, although Moslem Malays never eat this forbidden meat. Many Straits Chinese women prefer the Malay sarong to the Chinese *samfoo*. Even traditional wedding ceremonies blend Malay customs with Chinese, holding the ceremony at the bride's house, for instance, although Chinese tradition would have forbidden the bridegroom to enter her home.

Many of these Straits Chinese families were market gardeners or worked in rubber or spice plantations as well as in the tin industry. Singapore's first dealer in "motor spirit" was Chinese. His first month's sale of eight gallons (all in bottles) is quite a contrast to today's monthly gas-station business, servicing more than 265,795 motor vehicles. Others were traders and shopkeepers whose philanthropy helped develop Singapore. Tan Kim Seng, founder of a Malacca merchant dynasty, provided $13,000 to bring a water supply to the city, while Tan Tock Seng in 1844 donated $5,000 toward a hospital.

Listening to the radio today, you realize how difficult it is to generalize about more than 1.5 million citizens. The majority still speak their own dialects at home. Radio Sin-

CHINESE FAMILIES

gapura therefore adds to its programs in Mandarin (the standard Chinese taught in Singapore schools and understood by all educated Chinese) regular broadcasts in six other dialects.

If you want to see Old China, you go not to the families living in modern housing estates such as Queenstown, or luxury apartments in the Tanglin area, but to the narrow area along North Bridge Road and South Bridge Road. Yet here too the multiracial nature of the city is evident. Within Chinatown's boundaries there are both a mosque where many Indians worship and the city's oldest Hindu temple, Sri Mariamman.

In Chinatown, elderly gentlemen in the tunic and loose black trousers of their home province share the sidewalk with women and children in *samfoo*. This everyday Chinese costume includes a blouse fastened at the side and comfortable pajamalike trousers, usually of cool cotton material. The girls change out of the *samfoo* into trim uniform on schooldays, however, while their older sisters are already wearing the newest fashions, or are dressed in the *cheongsam*, a high-collared slit-sided dress favored in Hong Kong and Taiwan. Older ladies tend to wear black rather than colors, but old and young alike often carry their wealth on their wrists in the form of gold or jade bracelets.

LIVING IN SINGAPORE

Unlike the towering buildings of the housing estates, in which so many families of all races now live, the houses of Chinatown are small and crowded. Many of the old buildings are shop-houses, with a family business on the ground floor. Here you can find a son helping to grind herbs for Chinese medicine or working in the family motor-repair business or wrapping packets of tea. Behind this shop is space for the family. Upstairs are the cubicles, diminutive sleeping compartments in which ten people may sleep in a room ten feet by ten!

No wonder that you see so much activity on the sidewalks and in the streets of this section, with bamboo poles of laundry protruding from every available window. There is no room for cooking in an overcrowded cubicle, and for many residents, eating at outdoor stalls is the equivalent of the family dining table. Others patronize the hawker who advertises his wares by the rhythmical beating of a wooden stick on a hollow bamboo. Children take a midafternoon break and go to the stalls just outside the school gates for sweet drinks made from sugar cane, various kinds of beans, and cut fruits.

At the small restaurants and sidewalk stalls, every member of the hardworking Chinese family must help. You can see a ten-year-old boy chopping the vegetables, spices, and pork to be served with Chinese rice porridge. Another is

CHINESE FAMILIES

turning tasty pieces of beef on a charcoal grill, while a third helps serve customers at the family butcher shop, where roast pigs, smoked ducks, and even a large pig's head are on display. No wonder that a million pigs are slaughtered in Singapore every year!

In addition to pork *satay*, you can enjoy chicken with betel nuts, or *gulai ikan* (sweetfish curry), or hot prawns served with pineapple. Lots of coconut milk is used, as in curry-chicken's thick gravy of chili and spices. Curry and chili pepper bases are typical of the Straits Chinese food

The family butcher shop, Chinese style. On display are smoked duck, pig's head, and many cuts of pork.

A Chinese family spreads out chili peppers, ginger, beans, and eggplant for sale

that all Singapore enjoys, but various areas of China have contributed their specialties, such as Hokkien *mee*, a dish of noodles boiled with prawns, spices, and vegetables. Cantonese cooks are noted for their sweet-sour sauce. Hunan's spicy sauces and other foods were enjoyed by the long-ago court of the Chinese emperor. Today you can eat their "fried water-chicken," a translation of the Chinese term for "frog."

Chinese families are particularly fond of soup, although

CHINESE FAMILIES

only a few appreciate such traditional varieties as bat, snake, toad, and pig's brain. Black vinegar is served with shark's-fin soup, while other soups may be seasoned with ginger and coriander. Hokkien cooks make turtle soup, and all Chinese enjoy soup made from the edible birds' nests found in Indonesian caves.

Even the most modern Chinese families, who regularly serve toast, marmalade, and coffee at breakfast time, sometimes prefer a traditional breakfast of soup, such as pork broth. A businessman often pauses at a sidewalk eating stand to sample such delicacies. Instead of stopping at a coffeeshop for a snack, many people in Singapore prefer to eat such tidbits as Chinese balls of minced meat, mushrooms, or prawns wrapped in very thin pasta. At forty Singapore cents, these snacks, known as *tim sum*, make a delicious, quick, and inexpensive breakfast. Combined with a bowl of noodles, *tim sum* makes a hearty lunch.

Roadside stalls are Singapore's favorite cafés. Some, like those beside the Singapore River, where you enjoy *satay*, are busiest during office lunch hours. Others are night eating stalls, set up at regular locations, such as Orchard Road, where they are right across from the supermarket. Malay, Indian, European, and American families can be found there as well as Chinese.

You might not enjoy such Hakka specialties as fried

intestines of pig served with salted vegetables, or fried cow stomach. But the stalls also serve delicious Chinese desserts, ranging from the cold longans of Swatow and "white fungus" and lotus seeds of Hunan to melon seeds, almond bean curd, and sweet potatoes in a thick syrup. You might have a cool drink of bean juice, or carry away your drink of fruit juice in a plastic bag! And you could even buy a modernized version of an ancient Chinese drink, soy-bean milk. This was known in China two thousand years ago, but today's variety comes in bottles, with vitamins added.

After your refreshments, you could walk along nearby South Bridge Road, past the glittering stores of the goldsmiths with their thin gold bangles and earrings, jade rings, bracelets, and pendants. Nearby, or perhaps on Cross Street, you can watch the Chinese herbalist making up prescriptions that have been handed down unchanged from the Imperial Court of a thousand years ago. His son helps grind the roots and leaves, and can already identify such items as tiger's claws, rhinoceros horn, and ginseng, a root used as a tonic. There are jars of pearls to be ground up for complexion-whitening powder, and deer skulls with horns attached for the making of a medicine used in reducing fever. Side by side with these traditional cures there may be modern patent medicines. But today's Singapore newspapers carry advertisements for an ancient medicine:

In a Chinese medicine shop, a boy learns how to grind herbs and prepare traditional medicines

"Rhino-horn Fever Water," recommended also as "a cure for baby's measles"!

There are other links with China's past of thousands of years ago. A fortune-teller crouches with his two parrots, ready to send the bird in quest of your paper fortune. The birds will peck out a marked bamboo stick for about twenty Singapore cents. Another fortune-teller, perhaps at one of the temples, will shake a box of numbered bamboo pieces until one emerges; then he will read your fortune from a paper numbered to match the bamboo sticks. Other fortune-tellers read the lines of your hand or even marks on your face.

Although all schoolchildren in Singapore today learn to

LIVING IN SINGAPORE

read and write at least two languages, many older citizens do not know how to write the difficult Chinese characters, some of which require more than twenty strokes. So there are professional letter writers on the sidewalk, too, ready to write notes or even poems for a few cents. Other traditional Chinese services are offered in shops such as the charcoal dealer's. A wood carver applies fine gold leaf to a delicately carved sandalwood Buddha. Craftsmen in nearby shop-houses make bamboo blinds or lanterns or baskets.

The truly unique craftsman, though, is the paper maker. He specializes in the objects needed for Chinese funerals, using split bamboo and fine paper to construct houses,

Bilingual signs announce the office of a clan association, which sponsors welfare programs for its members

chests, cars, suits of clothes, and even effigies of servants to accompany the departed on his journey to the other world. This paper maker is only one part of Singapore's unusual funeral industry, a natural development in a culture that believes a funeral for anyone who has reached the age of sixty is a particularly happy occasion.

These are only some of the traditions transplanted from ancient China to modern Singapore. Signs saying "Clan Association," for instance, remind you that these associations or tongs have changed to meet the world of today. Once the focus for rivalry and even fighting, they have now become welfare organizations, which sponsor housing, schools, and medical facilities for clan members. The face of Singapore continues to change, too. Under the government's urban-renewal scheme, the hundred-year-old buildings of Chinatown will be pulled down to make way for modern multistoried flats that will also house families who now live in *kampongs*.

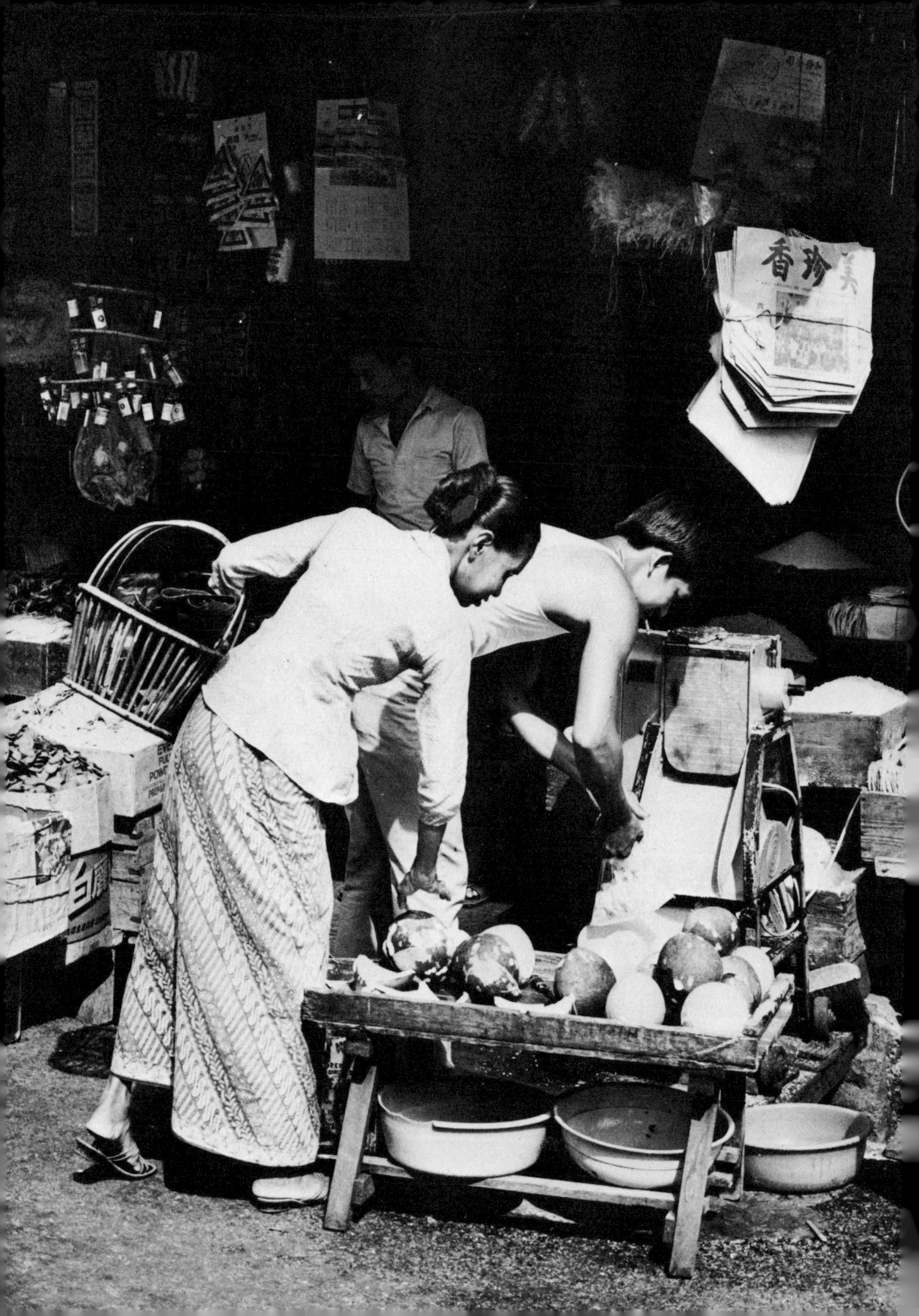
美珍香

4. The Malay Heritage

MALAYS lived on the island of Singapore centuries before the arrival of Sir Stamford Raffles, and you can visit the tomb of a fourteenth-century sultan in Singapore today. Malay is the national language of the Republic, yet not all of today's Malays are descended from the early residents. Many of the 14 percent of the Singaporeans classified as Malay are in fact more recent immigrants than some Chinese and Indian members of the community. They did not even travel to the city of Singapore from the mainland of the Malay Peninsula. Instead, they came from the islands of Indonesia, settling in areas of Singapore now named Java Road, Bali Lane, and so on.

A Malay housewife in *sarong kebaya* shops for coconut, used in many traditional dishes

LIVING IN SINGAPORE

Today's Malay citizens, like the Chinese, are found in all areas of the Republic's life. The first Malayan-born representative of the English monarch was Inche Yusof bin Ishak, who later became the first President of the Republic. Malays help move the cargoes through Singapore's port, they do much of the paperwork in government offices, and of course they teach in the schools. Their language is Standard Malay, and this (like Mandarin Chinese) was originally a court language. It can be understood by all the peoples of the Malay Peninsula, Singapore, and Indonesia, although Indonesia has its own language.

Malays are all called by their personal names, since they do not have surnames. They are called *bin* ("son of") or *binti* ("daughter of") their male parent. A brother and sister are Ali bin Abdullah and Meriam (Mariam) binti Abdullah. The girl's name will not change when she marries Hamid bin Amat, but will remain "Mariam, the daughter of Abdullah," even when her own daughter is born and called Fetima (Fatima) binti Hamid.

These names, like other elements of Malay life, follow Arabic and Islamic custom. The Malay marriage service, for instance, is conducted in Arabic. Funerals are held within six hours of death and, in contrast with the gay Chinese parades, are quiet occasions. The opening chapter of the Holy Book, the Koran, is read on the way to the

Modern touches in a stilt-supported *kampong*: corrugated iron roof, wire netting, and goggles for diving

graveyard, and conversation is forbidden. Other rules of conduct are part of the *adat* ("ancient custom") of long-ago Malay villagers, including the *orang laut* ("sea people") whose families welcomed Sir Stamford Raffles.

You can find a whole community preserving some of the ancient Malay ways right within sight of the modern docks, on the island of Pulau Brani. Here descendants of the *orang laut* live in typical houses built on stilts over the water. The streets of this village are narrow boardwalks connecting the houses. Traditionally, their roofs are made

47

LIVING IN SINGAPORE

of *attap,* the leaves of the swamp palm. Occasionally you can see women sewing leaves together over anchoring spines of the leaf. The framework of the house is bamboo, and walls are also made of *attap,* with a hinged flap for the window. Most of the homes on Pulau Brani, though, have substituted corrugated iron for the roof, and use board siding and modern window frames.

Visiting a village family, you see modern upholstered chairs—and there is more plastic, steel, and chromium than bamboo or palm. There is even a cabin cruiser tied up outside one house, and most of the housewives are quite famil-

A fish trap (*kelong*) is built in the ancient way near a Malay village. Nets are set out at night and hauled up in the morning.

THE MALAY HERITAGE

iar with the stores and markets of central Singapore. The children are just as much at home in the water as their long-ago ancestors, but today they put on underwater goggles and rubber fins before diving.

In spite of such modern touches, the *kelong* or fish trap of the Malays is still constructed in the traditional way, with *attap* thatch over a sturdy bamboo framework. As you go swimming off Changi or cruise in Singapore waters, you see many of these *kelongs*, and may even watch workmen constructing one within sight of giant modern oil tankers. There is a small house, and a row of fishing stakes stretch out into the water. At night, nets are lowered into the water, to be hauled up with a good catch in the morning.

Pulau Brani and the *kelongs* are two reminders of Singapore's Malay heritage. Malay *kampongs* (villages) can be found among the coconut groves and rubber plantations of the island, too. Some of the *kampong* houses are built on stilts, while others follow the style preferred by the Straits Chinese, and are built directly on the ground. But the *kampong* is fast disappearing from the city scene as such villages make way for blocks of new flats.

The modern housing-estate Malays include some of Singapore's police force and special constabulary, two thirds of whom are Malay. Others work on the Malaysian Railway or hold jobs as government clerks. For such workers, the colorful Malay wedding ritual may be observed only as a tourist attraction, and their only knowledge of the old ways of life comes from exhibits in the National Museum. Yet even these workers and their families are linked to the remote coastal villagers and fishermen by their religion, for all are followers of Islam.

They are Moslems, and they believe that Mohammed was the last of the prophets of God, whom they call Allah, "The Mighty One." Moslems do not drink alcohol or eat pork. The duties of their religion include the giving of alms. They must also pray five times each day. Instead of a priest, there is an imam, a man recognized for his scholarship and piety, to lead services. Men are called to prayer from the minaret of the mosques, but the voice calling "Allahu Akbar" today is often an electronic one (amplified).

Moslems gather at the Sultan Mosque and at smaller mosques in Singapore at noon every Friday. Men and boys over fourteen are all expected to attend, but women are not permitted in the main area of the mosque. If they wish to pray, they must wait until all the men have entered, and then stay behind a screen. Schools release Moslem boys from class early on Fridays, and it is a common sight to see these boys pausing in the schoolyard to wrap a sarong over their uniform shorts before hurrying off to prayers. It is the custom to enter the mosque only after ritual cleansing, and also to leave one's shoes at the door.

Worshipers first cleanse themselves (*left*), then leave their shoes on the steps before entering the Sultan Mosque

The dress of today's Malays shows the influence of the Moslem religion. Women are expected to be modestly dressed at all times. They used to go veiled, and this custom is preserved in the use of the *slendang*, although this is now simply a head covering or scarf. Until quite recently, all Moslem schoolgirls wore a long blouse or tunic, the *baju kurong*, over their sarongs, to cover them completely from the neck to below the knee. In 1969, however, entering Malay students began to wear regulation uniforms of blouses with short skirts or with gym tunics.

LIVING IN SINGAPORE

Malay office workers and teachers are among those wearing modern dresses and suits. At home and in the market, though, most women still prefer the *sarong kebaya*. The Malay sarong is a two-and-a-half yard length of cloth, a little over a yard wide. It is worn wrapped around the waist. Over this goes the *kebaya*, a close-fitting blouse.

The sarong is usually made of batik, the dyed cloth for which Malaysia and Java are noted. It may take ten hours or more to make one length of batik. The artist first outlines a design in wax and then dips the cloth repeatedly in dye, warming it to remove the wax as successive colors are

Malay boys in shorts, sarong, and *songkok* (the Malay cap) are on their way to the mosque

THE MALAY HERITAGE

applied. Traditional colors are those of vegetable dyes—brown, yellow, and blue—although modern designs from Malaysia's Kelantan are often in such bright colors as orange.

Malay men, too, wear distinctive clothes on special occasions, although they wear simple white shirts and dark slacks at work. At home, many change into a sarong knotted around the waist. Usually this is a length of tartan or checked-pattern material, rather than the batik preferred by women.

Because of the Moslem belief that pork is unclean, the meat in Malay meals is usually mutton—as in *khorma*, a very highly spiced mutton stew. Malays also enjoy goat meat. On ordinary occasions, fish is often on the menu. There is a "salad" of bean curd, prawns, and eggs with a peanut sauce. There are even "prawn crisps" (*keropok*), resembling an outsize potato chip. The Malay housewife cooks the same kinds of fish as her Chinese neighbors, adding her own favorite spices. Chili crab, for instance, is fried with chilies, beans, ginger, and garlic.

Many favorite Singapore dishes use coconuts. A popular dessert is *gula melaka* (*gula* is jaggery, the coarse brown sugar of palm sap, and *melaka* is the Malay way of saying Malacca). It is made with sago, melted palm sugar, and coconut cream. Another dessert is a mixture of yams, sago, and sweet potato in coconut milk. Coconut milk is an important ingredient in making curries and cakes. *Daging seronding* is sliced beef coated with grated coconut. There is even a Malay expression to describe people who keep too much to themselves: "Like frogs under a coconut shell." Familiar sights in the markets are Malay housewives buying grated coconut (often from a Chinese vendor) and groups of children enjoying glasses of coconut milk. No wonder that almost all of the fourteen million coconuts produced on the island are eaten locally!

Malay families, like the Chinese and Indians, also eat a great deal of rice. A favorite accompaniment for rice is either *sambal* or *blachan*. These are two varieties of prawn paste, made by pounding prawns and chilies and other seasonings together. Even in the poorest Malay home you will find that the mother teaches her daughter how to cook rice and how to make *blachan* or *sambal*, using the traditional pounding stone. However, instead of the well-scrubbed counter space of the new blocks of flats, the *kampong* housewife may make do with a piece of newspaper spread on the floor.

Like *satay*, many other Malay dishes are cooked over charcoal, but this fuel is expensive. Some *kampong* Malays salvage pieces of wood instead, and even the youngest boy learns how to chop wood for the cooking fire. Over this fire

THE MALAY HERITAGE

the housewife prepares cooked rice (*nasi*) to be eaten at every meal. Rice also forms the basis of many Malay dishes. A favorite school lunch with Malay, Indian, and Chinese students alike is *nasi lemak*, rice mixed with coconut milk, chili, and *ikan bilis* (anchovy). Everyone enjoys *nasi bryani*, too, an Indian specialty, and *nasi goreng*, fried rice with shrimp, sliced beef, or mutton (Chinese families prefer pork), and eggs. The names of many other dishes also tell you how they are cooked, with *goreng* (to fry) and *rebus* (to boil or steam) being the most common.

Of course you might find these dishes on any table in Singapore. Just as the *Nyonya* (Straits Chinese) borrowed from their Malay neighbors, so today's Malays have borrowed from their Chinese and Indian friends. Indian curries have been brought to Malay kitchens as *nasi kari* (curry and rice). And when you visit an Indian family, you will not be surprised if you are served Malay delicacies or such Chinese dishes at Hokkien *mee*. The only differences are some of the ingredients.

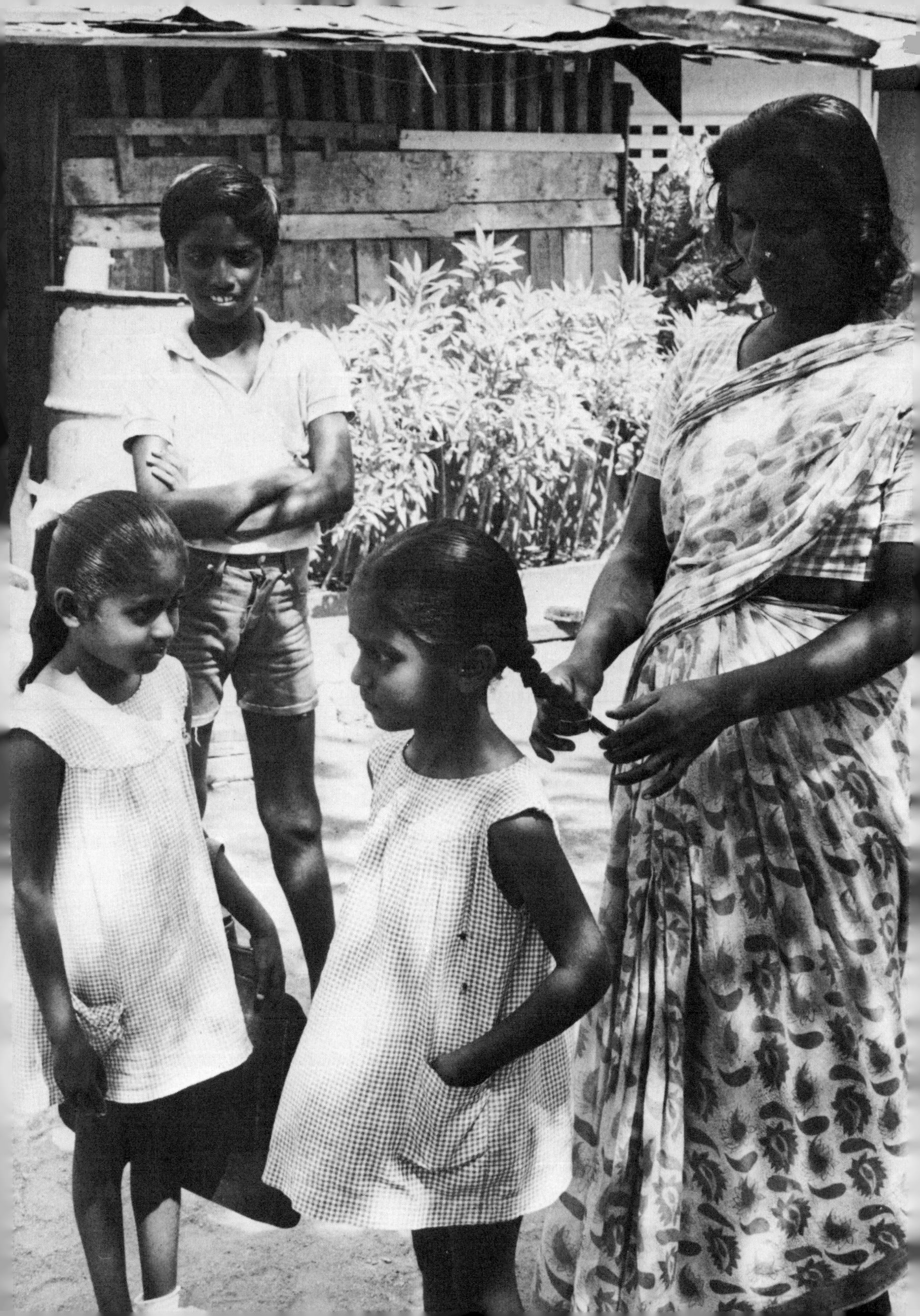

5. Indian Families

TRADERS from India visited the Malay Peninsula centuries ago. Scholars say that Indians settled near Kedah on the Malay Peninsula at the point where ships waited for the monsoon to change, and that Gujarati merchants brought the Islamic faith to the Malays. Over many decades, the Malays adopted some Indian customs. They also added Tamil and Hindustani words to their vocabulary. But modern residents of Singapore cannot trace their ancestry to these pioneers.

Malacca, the ancient trading center on the Malay coast above Singapore, was even an Indian missionary center for a while. Malacca was also linked with Temasek by the Hindu prince Parameswara, who fled from that "Sea

Hindus living in a Malay village continue to wear saris and to dress their hair in Indian fashion

LIVING IN SINGAPORE

Town" in the fourteenth century, settled in Malacca, and became a Moslem.

Singapore's direct links with Indian culture came in other ways: through the early administration under the East India Company, and through immigrant workers. Late in the nineteenth century, Indian workers came under contracts that the Indian government negotiated with planters of coffee and rubber and with European tin-mine owners in the Malay States and in Singapore. Such indentured labor ended in 1914, however. The most recent immigrants include businessmen and ex-servicemen who chose to be demobilized from the British armed forces in Singapore.

Only 8 percent of today's Singaporeans are Indian or Pakistani, yet the range of their dress, occupations, and religions is as great as that to be found in the subcontinent itself. A single Hindu family may include a grandmother born in Kerala State, a father from Madras, with mother and daughters born in Singapore. These women all prefer the graceful sari to modern Western dress.

Men from states bordering the Bay of Bengal often wear *dhoti*, a length of white fabric twisted around the waist and between the legs, and then tucked in at the waist. Some of the Indians in Singapore wear a sarong, calling it a *kaili*. Pakistani men may wear *salwar* (close-fitting trousers) and *kameez* (tunic).

INDIAN FAMILIES

The sari worn by women is a six-yard length of fabric that is carefully draped to form a long dress, with one end sometimes used as a head covering The fabric may be longer, but it is never sewn or pinned. It is, however, draped in many different styles. Simple cotton saris cost only a few Singapore dollars, but a sari embroidered in gold thread, and even jeweled, costs over three hundred

Indian women gossip outside their homes. The Sikh woman in the background wears tunic slit partway up the sides and a head scarf

LIVING IN SINGAPORE

Singapore dollars. The sari is worn over a short blouse, the *choli*.

Sikh women dress in a style similar to that of the Moslem Pakistanis. They wear a long tunic, slit partway up at the sides, over trousers that fit closely at the ankles. They also wear a head scarf similar to that of Moslem women, and often dress their hair in long braids. Like all Indian women and girls, they have beautifully glossy dark hair, combed with perfumed oil.

The wife of a wealthy Singapore businessman or professional man might prefer to wear Italian silk prints. But for parties she still wears a fine silk sari over a sheer *choli*, as well as diamonds, and the delicate gold necklaces and pendants for which Indian jewelers are famous. Her seven- and eleven-year-old daughters wear cottons and drip-dry clothes, except for special occasions, when they wear tunic and pants similar to those of the Pakistanis. One daughter studies in an English preparatory school; the other attends one of Singapore's convents, for this family worships at a Roman Catholic church. Both daughters study classical Indian dancing, yet they prefer to spend their time playing Ping-Pong or horseback riding. Their thirteen-year-old brother enjoys Rugby football and squash.

Visiting such a family, you might imagine yourself in an English country home. The maid wheels in a tea cart con-

Young Indian girls may don tunic and trousers for special occasions, but ordinarily they dress in Western clothes. Women wear the graceful sari.

taining a silver service and an assortment of dainty sandwiches and pastries. You soon discover, however, that this is afternoon tea Singapore style. The maid is wearing the Malay sarong, and the hostess is wearing a silk sari as she entertains her American guest. Other Indian families enjoy tea spiced with cinnamon, or served with lime juice instead of milk, and you may find a laborer's daughter serving her parents cups of strong, very sweet tea with lots of milk and sugar.

Among the most distinctive Indian families are the Sikhs, all of whom have the name Singh, meaning "lion." Many are *jaga* (watchmen) guarding Singapore's banks and office buildings. Their string beds (*charpoy*) are

LIVING IN SINGAPORE

neatly propped against the wall during business hours. Coming originally from the eastern Punjab, they used to have a reputation as great warriors. Sikh men wear iron bangles around their wrists. They never cut their hair but wear turbans, while their young sons wear their hair in a topknot that is covered with a small piece of fabric. Sikhs retain this turban even if they join Singapore's military or police forces, and older boys wear their turbans in the classroom.

Near Collyer Quay you may see Chettiar moneylenders, usually identified by their white *dhoti* and long tunic. They are descendants of Hindus in Madras. In the port area, there are Indian Moslem workers from the Malabar Coast, wearing sarongs like those of the Malays. Other areas have traditionally supplied workers for certain occupations. The finest gem cutters are jewelers from Ceylon (the island off

A Sikh father and son. The boy's hair will never be cut and is worn in a covered topknot until he is old enough for the traditional turban. A white skull cap identifies a passerby as a *haji*—a Moslem who has made a pilgrimage to Mecca.

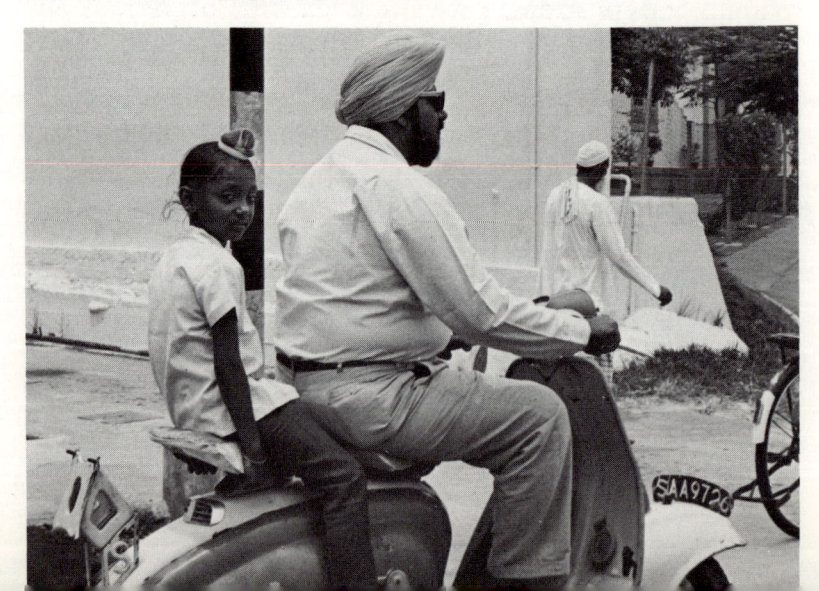

INDIAN FAMILIES

India's southern tip). Merchants from Bombay sell spices, silks, and groceries. But most of Singapore's Indian and Pakistani doctors, businessmen, and office workers do not wear distinctive clothes. Their suits, smartly tailored in Singapore, are indistinguishable from those worn on Madison Avenue or on London's Bond Street.

As many as two thirds of Singapore's Indian families are Tamil-speaking people whose ancestors lived in southern India or Ceylon. Many of them are laborers or unskilled workers, although some can be found in banking, government, and medicine, or working for the hotels or in railway jobs. Others are workers in the power station or in the brick factory.

Many Tamil families are Hindus. A Hindu home includes a family altar where a lamp burns throughout the day. Family members raise their hands in prayer and burn sweet-smelling sandalwood before its images, which frequently include Ganesha, the elephant-headed deity associated with good fortune.

Hindus worship Brahma the Creator, Vishnu the Preserver (or Protector), and Shiva the Destroyer who also Re-Creates. One of Vishnu's incarnations was as the Buddha, and so there is a small Buddha on the family altar, too. Occasionally there is even a text with a picture of Jesus, for Hindus accept the divinity of the gods of other religions as well.

Gandhi and Jesus are both given places on this Hindu family's altar

Wayside shrines (*kovils*) may shelter only the image of a single cow. Cows are sacred in India, and for more than three thousand years Hindus have refused to eat beef, although milk and other products from the cow are used in various religious ceremonies.

Visiting Sri Mariamman, Singapore's oldest Hindu temple, you enter beneath a soaring ornamental tower. Taking off your shoes, you may then enter the sacred precincts. In

INDIAN FAMILIES

small detached pavilions and in alcoves of the main temple, as well as painted on the roof, you will see many deities, including Durga, the Warrior Goddess, with her lion, fierce Kali painted in brilliant colors and with tongue protruding, and Mariamman.

A great candlestick holds 108 candles, and beyond is the sanctuary, where chanting priests raise lamps before the altars. The air is perfumed with sandalwood. Sacred ash from the altar fires, sandalwood paste, and holy water, as well as *kungumum* (reddish paste used to mark the forehead) are distributed to the worshipers. You hear the sounds of ancient musical instruments such as the *nagas-*

Singapore musicians play ancient instruments at a Hindu temple

waram (windpipe) and the *mirdangam* (a percussion instrument).

Besides the many Hindus and Moslems of Singapore's Indian and Pakistani population, there are Christians—Protestants as well as Roman Catholics. There are also Parsis, who follow the teachings of Zoroaster, a Persian religious leader of about eight thousand years ago. Some Indians have Portuguese names, reminders of the days when the Portuguese Empire stretched around the world.

The foods enjoyed by these families are as varied as their ancestors. Most of them eat a great deal of rice, and in many families it is the custom to eat only two meals a day. The first meal is in the morning, and the other is taken in late afternoon. Other families prefer an English-style breakfast, with cereal and cream, a boiled egg, and strong tea served with plenty of milk. They also enjoy such tropical fruits as papaya and mango. A typical Indian dinner would be curry. This is not made with a simple curry powder, however, for each housewife prefers to blend her own spices.

Many Indian dishes are served cold, but with bowls of warm Patna rice or with various kinds of bread. Everyone enjoys *chapatties*, a bread made with wheat flour. These are cooked on a heavy metal pan, sometimes over a charcoal fire. *Ghee* (clarified butter) is an essential ingredient

At a Hindu temple, young worshipers share a feast served on banana leaves

for Indian cookery. It may be used to fry bread, or mixed with coconut milk and spices to make saffron rice.

Often Indian families join the crowds at Singapore's outdoor eating stalls, where they enjoy *murtabah*, a kind of flaky dough stuffed with minced meat and onions. Many families from northern India enjoy chicken, goat meat, and lamb. They prefer lightly spiced dishes, made with saffron and delicate herbs instead of the hot chilies so popular in other areas. Some Hindus are vegetarians, and they go to "Brahmin" restaurants in the Serangoon Road area. These restaurants serve food on banana leaves, just as

67

it is served at the Hindu temples. A favorite dish is *avial*, made with boiled vegetables such as squash, potatoes, and peas mixed with yoghurt, coconut, and spices. The food served on a banana leaf is eaten without spoons or forks: you use your right hand only. At home, many vegetarian families eat *dhal*, a lentil soup. These foods may be accompanied by a glass of pepper water. Other popular drinks are coconut juice and buttermilk (*lassi* to northern Indians, but *thairu* in the south).

Near the vegetarian restaurants live many Indian families, and you can see boys wearing the iron bangles and long hair that identify them as Sikhs. There are Hindu girls wearing earrings of fine gold and delicate glass bangles, while their mothers wear diamond nose jewels and sometimes rings on their toes. The women are mostly in saris or in the long tunics and trousers of Sikh and Moslem women, but the children dress much as they would in America.

Invited to enter one of these homes, you are welcomed in the traditional Indian way. Grandfather and one of the girls stand in the doorway, raising their hands to their lips, as they bow their heads and say, *"Namaste,"* the common Indian greeting. This house is gay with brightly patterned curtains, plastic and paper flowers, colored plastic chains, and brilliantly painted figures of gods and goddesses on a shelf.

INDIAN FAMILIES

In a small *kampong* near the port of Singapore you can find an Indian family living next door to Malays. Instead of the plump pillows and familiar wooden beds of other Indian homes, this family uses rush sleeping mats. At night these are placed on the wooden sleeping platform.

In many such families, ancient traditions and modern ways exist side by side. The children go barefoot in the house, following centuries-old Indian custom, but they are watching a Tamil film of Aladdin's adventures on TV. They are studying English at school, and have no difficulty reading the subtitles. Saroja is learning to prepare chilies, watching her mother use the grinding stone that has been used in Indian kitchens for hundreds of years.

Little Muthumari speaks the family's Tamil dialect at home, but in spite of her father's low income she is going to a nearby kindergarten where she speaks English with Malay and Chinese children. She will soon be six years old, and then she will enter the public schools of Singapore. She will share the same strict upbringing of all Indian girls, rarely leaving the house as she grows older. Yet she will study three languages, and in secondary school she will study today's technical subjects. She will be prepared to share in the life of modern industrial Singapore, and will bring her rich Indian heritage to share with Chinese and Malay friends.

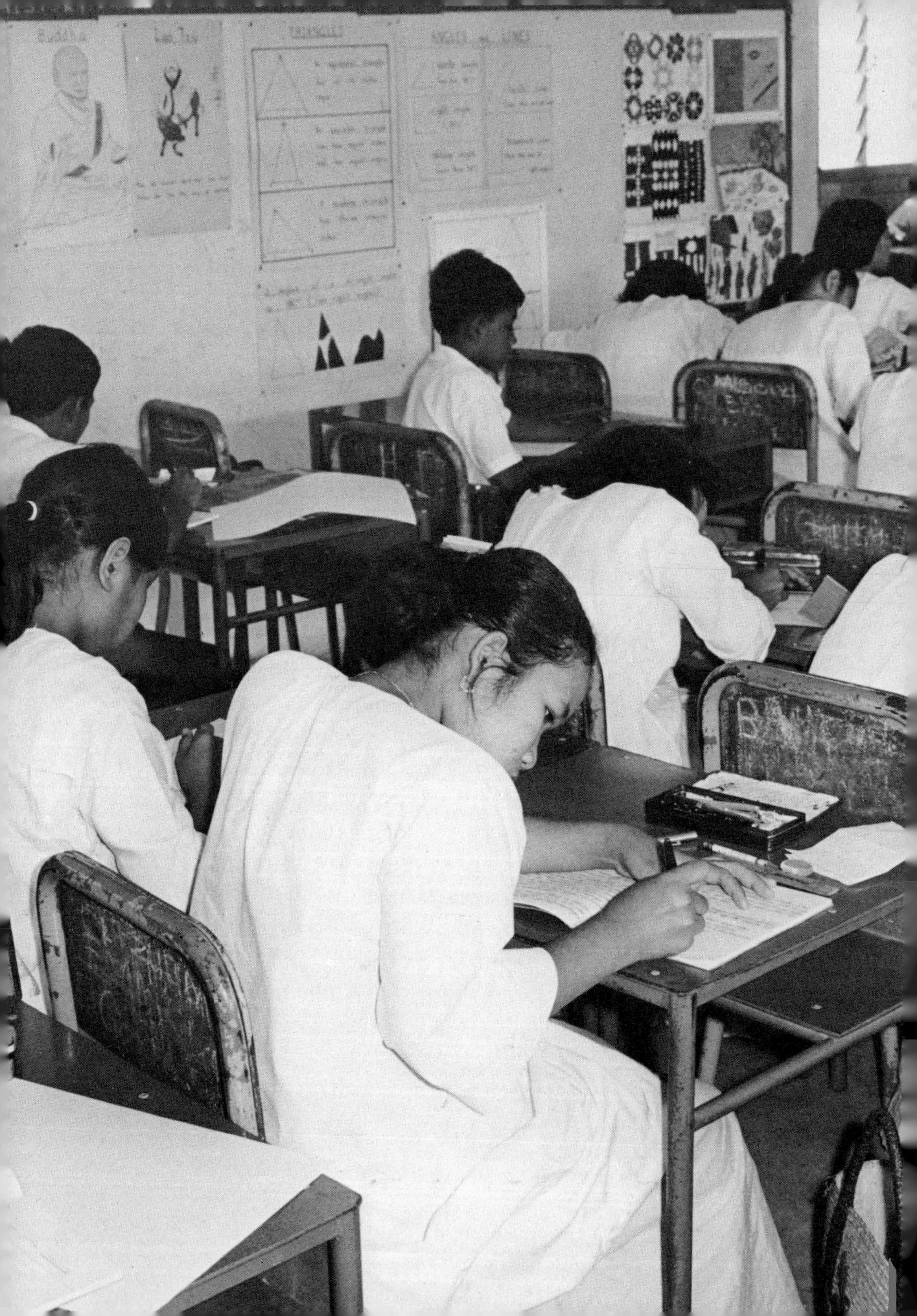

6. Schools for Everyone

CHINESE, Malay, Indian, English—the cultures that have made the Republic of Singapore are all to be found in the city's modern classrooms. You may find a mathematics teacher speaking Tamil and writing problems in this script, or a science teacher wearing a sari and instructing in English. You can see pupils bending over their desks practicing calligraphy by copying the Chinese ideograms written by their teacher, who wears a *cheongsam* and speaks with the musical tones of Mandarin. Singapore provides four separate language streams for the varying backgrounds of its citizens, and parents choose any of these official languages for their children's education.

Moslem students in a Malay-stream school also study Buddha and Lao-Tzu, as shown by their classroom posters

LIVING IN SINGAPORE

Almost a third of Singapore's total budget is spent on education to permit students to study in English (the most popular choice), Chinese, Malay, or Tamil. In addition to 270 government schools, there are 241 government-aided schools and 62 private schools, some providing education for Singapore's foreign residents. The private schools include a Dutch school, a Japanese school, and a Gujarati school. At the American School, a thousand students from twenty-nine countries ranging from Australia to Yugoslavia (774 are American) are taught by seventy teachers from eleven nations. The pattern at the American School follows the educational pattern of schools in the United States, but even here the curriculum has a distinctively Singaporean flavor. Pythons and monkeys appear in the biology lab, there are field trips to Malacca and to festivals such as Deepavali, and there are lessons in Malay from a *kampong* leader.

Singapore is a secular state, but special provision is made for the Moslem students. Boys are released from school early on Fridays so that they can join their fathers at the mosque when the noon call to prayer sounds. Many Malay boys and girls also attend Moslem religious school for instruction in the Koran. So important is such religious instruction that even the poorest parents set aside money for the extra lessons.

Students of many races lunch on noodles, soup, and cola drinks at the school "tuck shop"

About one fourth of all Singapore's citizens are at present students in primary and secondary schools. Although school is not compulsory, primary education is free. If students fail to graduate at the end of the six years, they must pay a small school fee for any additional primary study.

There are still many one-language-stream schools, but more and more students are meeting in one of Singapore's integrated schools. At the 127 integrated schools, there are two or three parallel language streams. There might be classes in Tamil and in English, but the English classes would include students from all of Singapore's linguistic backgrounds. A Chinese bank clerk, an Indian storekeeper, and a Malay port worker might all prefer to have their children fluent in English, especially since that is the language of government and business.

Whatever stream they are in, all students mingle freely during sports and at the school tuck shop. The words "tuck shop" are another reminder of English influence, but the foods on sale during the students' twenty-minute breaks have little in common with traditional English sweets. You can buy various kinds of nuts and seeds and even shredded dried plum in packages costing a few cents. Hot dishes costing from ten to thirty Singapore cents include *mee rebus*, a dish of noodles mixed with spices, chilies, and bean sauce.

At a typical integrated school, some Tamil-stream students study such subjects as biology, physics, mathematics, and history in their own language. Entering students, however, are now given extra practice in English through mathematics and science classes, and soon these subjects will be taught only in English. There are more girls than boys in the Tamil stream, because of Indian tradition. Girls are expected to marry and stay at home, while boys must go out into the business world, where they need fluent English. Some of the Tamil boys in English-stream classes

SCHOOLS FOR EVERYONE

do not even take Tamil as their second language, although their parents speak it at home. Instead, they study either Malay or the difficult Mandarin.

In an English-stream class, you will see a Sikh boy whose second language is Malay. At the end of his year in Primary Six he can read Malay *pantuns*, quatrains in which the first couplet contains a hint of the meaning made specific in the second couplet. A girl who takes Mandarin as her second language is reading familiar Western stories, including *Cinderella* and *Alice in Wonderland*, but they are written in Chinese ideograms.

Whichever language they choose, all Singapore students must learn a second language from the time they enter primary school after their sixth birthday. In their third year of school, they add the national language, Malay, which everyone studies for at least one period a week. It is not at all uncommon to find a student who speaks a Chinese dialect at home, yet studies English as his first language and Malay as the second. Like the Sikh and Tamil boys, he is preparing for the business world. But whichever language he chooses, the student spends hours studying it. Even in his first year of primary school, he spends 210 minutes a week on his second language. By Primary Six he takes four hours each of his first and second languages, and thirty-five minutes of Malay.

Singapore's school year begins in January and ends in

The turban and iron bangle identify this boy as a Sikh, but he is studying Malay verses in an English-stream school

early November. Students in the primary schools, who take turns attending morning and afternoon sessions in alternate years, have to be at school by 7:45. A boy in Primary One might attend classes from 7:45 to 12:45, while his sister in Primary Six would begin her school day at 1 P.M. Even the youngest student spends twenty hours and fifty minutes a week in the classroom—only two hours of this time allotted to physical education and assembly. Those in Primary Six have twenty-four hours and ten minutes a week in school, and their physical education and assembly time is cut to one hour and forty minutes.

SCHOOLS FOR EVERYONE

Extracurricular activities and most of the sports programs are scheduled for Saturday mornings, but it is a wonder that any student finds time for such extras. There is a Primary School Leaving Examination to be passed before students move on to secondary school, an exam requiring hours of preparation and review. After six years of primary grades, there are two years of secondary school. Some students leave school at the end of Secondary Two, but others remain for another two years and take the Cambridge Examinations in late November. Some spend an additional two years studying for the Higher School Certificate, in preparation for university studies.

The two years of Secondary One and Two used to be specialized, with students choosing academic, technical, or commercial curricula. They are now put in a common curriculum for all four language streams. The government recognized the need for more technical students and for domestic science to "benefit future citizens of the Republic," and they decided that by 1972 Singapore's educational system would be completely geared to industrial needs. In government and government-aided secondary schools, 75 percent of the students (all the boys and half of the girls) study technical subjects. Girls studying technical subjects take two periods of domestic science as well. These subjects—metalwork and woodwork, or metalwork

Students leave a school operated by Hokkien (Chinese) clan association at the end of the day

and basic electricity, and domestic science—are normally taught outside the regular school hours.

Students of thirteen and fourteen spend at least twenty-five hours and twenty minutes every week studying science, technical drawing, mathematics, history, geography, and three languages (first and second languages, and two periods of the national language). This time includes three hours of physical education and assembly. But after regular school hours and on Saturdays, the students gather on the school grounds for sports programs and for varied activities that range from ballet and bugle-and-fife bands to *taekwando* (the Korean art of self-defense). They also prepare for the annual Youth Festival.

SCHOOLS FOR EVERYONE

Although the usual school-leaving age is sixteen, about a hundred boys and girls from twelve to sixteen now work in industry. With a certificate of registration from the Commissioner of Labour they can hold such jobs as rubber-sheet strippers and sock packers. Before their twelfth birthday, children may not entertain for profit, but thirty or so between the ages of twelve and seventeen are employed as musicians, and as actors and actresses in the *wayang* troupes.

Students who fail to pass the various examinations or who for some reason must go to work at the end of their primary schooling or after two years of secondary school can still get quite good jobs. Sometimes they take a two-year vocational course, followed by an examination. Or they qualify for special training, perhaps to follow their fathers' occupations. For instance, a three-month fishing course teaches fishing, repair and construction of gear, navigation and seamanship, engine repair and maintenance, and shipbuilding and repair, with two months of lectures and of workshop in both Malay and Chinese, and one month's practical experience at sea. Other classes meet the needs of specialized groups, such as girls who want to follow their mothers' craft of bead embroidery. Lectures for this course are entirely in Chinese.

LIVING IN SINGAPORE

Those who wish advanced education may train as teachers at the Teachers' Training College, as one of more than two thousand students, or become one of the sixty or so students earning a degree at the University of Singapore's School of Education. This university has undergraduate and graduate courses in many fields, including law and medicine. It was originally known as Raffles College of Arts and Science. Its first principal, in the 1920's, was Sir Richard Winstedt. His dictionaries have helped thousands of Malay students to learn English as well as to study their own language. Later the college joined King Edward VII College of Medicine, first as part of the University of Malaya, then becoming the University of Singapore in 1962.

Chinese students can complete their education in Mandarin by attending Nanyang University in Jurong, where two thousand students take courses in arts, science, and commerce, and where even the buildings are in Chinese style. Ngee Ann Technical College, founded by the Ngee Ann Kongsi, gives courses in Chinese, Malay, engineering, and home economics. The Singapore Technical Institute and Singapore Polytechnic give specialized courses too.

Holders of the Higher School Certificate or of the School Certificate can take all sorts of jobs in government or private service. Those who have not gone beyond Secondary Three may work in offices, in the police force, as proofreaders, as lifeguards, and as dental assistants.

There are mostly girls in this mathematics class taught in Tamil. Boys prefer English as a more useful language.

Even students who do not graduate have opportunities for specialized training, as in the Ministry of Labour's Hotel and Catering Training Center. There is also a training ship, *Singapura,* to prepare boys for the merchant marine. But the majority of these special programs are designed to find workers for the growing industries of Singapore, as the city manufactures its own goods instead of depending on trade for its major income. Whatever job they choose, though, the new Singapore citizens will all be bilingual as a result of their training in the city's schools. Their new understanding of science, technology, languages, and human relations will help the port founded by Sir Stamford Raffles grow into the new industrial nation of Asia.

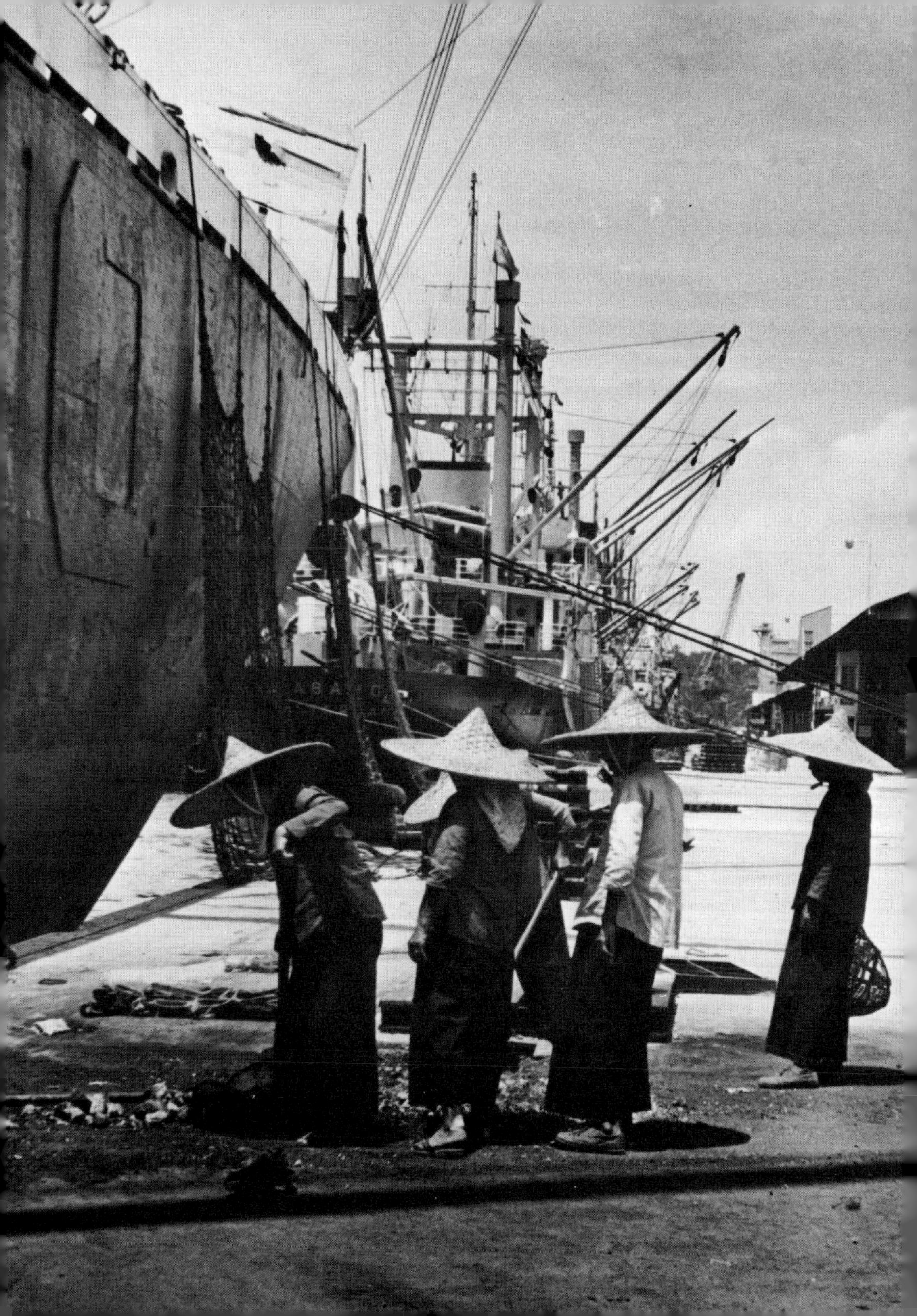

7. The Port and Industry

SINGAPORE today is the world's fourth-busiest port. More than ten thousand full-time workers keep six billion dollars' worth of imports flowing into lighters, across wharves, and onto waiting trucks and railroad cars, while four billion dollars' worth of raw materials and manufactured goods are being exported in a single year. This port is part of the city of Singapore. Yet it also forms its own community, with free housing and medical services for its workers, its own recreation club where you can play English cricket or Malay *sepak takraw,* and a colorful population that includes the descendants of Indonesian, Malay,

Women workers help keep the goods flowing through the Port of Singapore

Sailing vessels still ply Singapore waters as in centuries past

Chinese, Indian, and English seafarers of the sixteenth century.

When the Sultan of Johore and the East India Company signed their treaty in 1819, it was the result of Sir Stamford Raffles' insistence that the island would make an excellent trading center. At that time, ships traveled from China down the east coast of the Malay Peninsula on the northeast monsoon and returned when the monsoon changed. India merchants sailed east with the southwest winds. Four-thousand-foot Kedah Peak, regarded as a mountain

THE PORT AND INDUSTRY

home of the gods, and visible thirty miles at sea, was their landfall. They waited for the monsoon to change in an area near present-day Kedah, while other traders met at a halfway point and transshipped their merchandise across the narrow Malay Peninsula.

Gold, ivory, camphor, sandalwood—the earliest trade included all the goods that fifteenth- and sixteenth-century explorers had hoped to find in the Indies. Singapore lay midway between the porcelains, silks, and pearls of China and the riches of India, as well as being close to the In-

The Port of Singapore, where more than thirty berths provide facilities for the city's growing trade

LIVING IN SINGAPORE

donesian islands with their cloves, cinnamon, and pepper. From the Banda Islands came nutmeg, from the Moluccas, or Spice Islands, cloves. Timor sent sandalwood, and Sumatra shipped gold and camphor. The Bugis ships brought spices, gold dust, and coffee from the eastern archipelago.

All of these goods still flow through the port of Singapore, more than 17 percent of the trade being with West Malaysia. Japan, the United Kingdom, the United States, and China also account for much of Singapore's trade. But new goods have been added to those originally exchanged here. Now almost 7 percent of Singapore's imports is crude oil from Kuwait. Raw materials, including coffee, copra (dried coconut meat and source of coconut oil), and rubber are brought to Singapore from neighboring countries and reexported after processing, sorting, and grading. Manufactured goods from all over the world, including foodstuffs, machinery, and textiles, are unloaded at Singapore wharves, many in the Free Trade Zone, mostly for the countries of Southeast Asia. But since the 1960's, you also see the products of Singapore's own factories being loaded for export.

Not all of this cargo is handled by the Port of Singapore Authority's giant cranes, modern forklifts, and wharfside godowns, however. About one fourth is still carried ashore by lighters (*tongkangs*) that service ships in the Roads

THE PORT AND INDUSTRY

(the area of safe anchorage). Some of this cargo is still landed along the Singapore River, where many godowns remain just as they were built a century ago. Thousands of casual laborers work in this area, although they are not included in the count of PSA employees, since they are hired by private contractors.

On any afternoon in Singapore you can walk along the banks of the river and watch small lighters discharging their cargo into godowns. Until 1850, all cargo was worked here, and the workers nimbly scurrying down gangplanks with sacks of coffee on their heads today are little different from those of a hundred years ago. Then, such crops as coffee, pepper, and sago were still growing on the island of

Workers unload Indonesian pepper from a *tongkang*, complete with traditional painted eyes. Note the auto tires used as fenders.

LIVING IN SINGAPORE

Singapore itself, and Orchard Road took its name from the neighborhood's orchards, nutmeg trees, and spice gardens.

You can still enjoy the aroma of exotic eastern spices, but today's port is very different from the tiny settlement that welcomed a once-a-year junk carrying rice and textiles from China to exchange for the gambier of early plantation owners, or for mirrors and copper brought to Singapore from the Mediterranean. Since 1824, the net registered tonnage of ships entering and leaving the port has increased from 35,000 to 130 million. By 1835, several dozen vessels were in port at one time. Today, cargo liners and passenger vessels from all over the world sail in and out of the port. Thousands of coastal vessels, such as Chinese junks, dhows from Hadramaut, and small Malay *koleks*, carry cargoes for the immediate area. A Russian ship loads rubber for Eastern Europe, while one of the year's 800 American vessels discharges brake fluid and tinplate. One of the year's 2,640 Japanese ships discharges cotton fabric, watches, and steel before loading rubber and spices. In a single year, more than 17,000 vessels from sixty-seven nations call at this port.

Raffles would be amazed at the variety of goods handled by the port that grew out of his trading post. Some shipments weigh only a few pounds, including precious cargoes of edible birds' nests gathered in the caves of In-

THE PORT AND INDUSTRY

donesia, Thailand, and Borneo for gourmets around the world. There are also bulk shipments of latex, totaling 47,000 tons a year. One ship can carry a million dollars' worth of this liquid rubber in its tanks. The year's exports also include 33,000 tons of coconut oil, while the West African oil palms of the area produce more than 110,000 tons of palm oil. Coffee from Indonesia, timber, copra, and canned pineapples from the Malay Peninsula—these are only a few of the exports. In terms of worldwide production, however, three of the most important commodities handled by the port of Singapore are pepper, rubber, and tin.

More than one third of the world's pepper crop is marketed through Singapore today. Rubber and tin are even more closely connected with the growth of Singapore, for the great-grandfathers of many of today's Singapore citizens came from China or from India to work on the rubber plantations or in the tin mines. Railroads and highways that now link the cities of the Malay Peninsula were originally constructed for access to rubber and tin.

The modern rubber industry of the entire Malay Peninsula owes its beginnings to Singapore and to the Englishman who cultivated the first seeds in 1877 in Singapore's own Botanic Gardens. Only after seven years can the tree be tapped, by making a slash in its trunk. A container catches the sap that oozes out, to be shipped as latex (liquid rubber), in sheets of coagulated rubber, in thin sheets of crepe rubber, or in heavier, firmly pressed sheets.

By the early years of the twentieth century, the development of the automobile brought a demand for rubber tires. By the 1920's, over 50 percent of the world's rubber came from West Malaysia, much of it shipped through the Port of Singapore.

Tin was being produced long before Sir Stamford Raffles' arrival. It was exported to China from the mines of Perak and used as "silver" on joss sticks, the thin sticks of sandalwood paste burned in Chinese temples and also used in praying at home altars. After 1810, when the process of sealing tin cans was perfected, canners in the United Kingdom wanted tin for preserving luxury foods. In the United States, it was needed for canning meat and fish during the Civil War. Thus, tin smelting became Singapore's first industry. Tin ore was shipped from the mines to the tin smelter on Singapore's island of Pulau Brani. Now, one third of the world's tin comes from West Malaysia, much of it from the Kinta Valley. Tin is also shipped to Singapore from Thailand and Indonesia. But none comes from Singapore's own "Hill of Tin," Bukit Timah, the island's 581-foot-high point.

So closely is the economy of the area tied to rubber and tin that even today fluctuations on the world market can

A Malay port worker poses with his bright-eyed family

affect daily living costs. Newspapers always carry the latest prices. Malay tin is also blended with antimony and copper to make the area's pewterware. Other minerals passing through the port include bauxite, iron ore, tungsten, and copper concentrates.

All these goods are only a small part of the tonnage handled in the Port of Singapore each year. In 1969, about 77 percent of the cargoes consisted of mineral oils as distinct from vegetable oils, such as palm oil and coconut oil. Sev-

The island of Pulau Bukom houses a modern oil refinery and storage tanks

eral companies have refineries and storage units in the port area. One processes up to 20,000 barrels of crude oil per day. In the new Jurong area, another company has a capacity of 950,000 imperial gallons a day, with giant hoses permanently installed at the dock for supplying fuel oil to ships.

The major center of Singapore's oil industry, and the largest installation in the Far East, is the island of Pulau Bukom. Twenty-three years after the Suez Canal opened, the tanker *Murex* brought bulk kerosine from Russia for lo-

THE PORT AND INDUSTRY

cal distribution and for Bangkok. Oil for the lamps of Borneo, Siam, Singapore, and Sumatra was stored on Pulau Bukom. Tankers bringing kerosine from Russia carried rice, jute, and other Asian products to Europe. The demands for fuel increased as the first automobiles came to the island of Singapore. Then came planes. An early model was eaten by ants before it could be uncrated, but today's aircraft handle 18,000 metric tons of freight at Singapore International Airport per year, and have added jet fuel to the products of Pulau Bukom. Today's vessels bring six million tons of liquid petroleum gas, aviation fuel, diesel fuel, and other oils to Singapore every year.

The 150-acre island once known as Freshwater Island had to expand. Ships converting from coal burning to oil burning in the 1920's needed more and more fuel. By that time, gasoline was being imported from Sumatra and Borneo, and paraffin wax from Borneo and Java. And so hills were flattened and other areas filled until the island had spread to 280 acres. Now every day about two thousand workers commute to Pulau Bukom.

Their work supplies Southeast Asia and even Japan, Australia, and New Zealand with fuel oil. Now 130 tanks store 1.5 million tons of oil for refining, blending, and redistributing in a 20-million-ton trade that includes insecticides, liquid petroleum gas, solvents, and 100,000 tons of bitumen

LIVING IN SINGAPORE

a year. Tankers carrying more than 200,000 tons are almost routine, although in 1960 no tanker of even half that capacity had been launched.

The Pulau Bukom Refinery was the first of Singapore's "Pioneer Industries," in 1961, as the government encouraged its citizens to offer goods not previously available or not available in sufficient quantity for the modern city's needs. Yet even while such new industries developed, the ancient trade went on too. Although the center of the barter trade was recently moved from Telok Ayer Basin to a section of Jurong, as many as three thousand coastal vessels still bring over a million tons of goods, and these craft look much like those of two hundred years ago. Today, you see other vessels in the Telok Ayer Basin, lighters that have brought ashore cargoes originating in China, Hong Kong, and Taiwan.

Singapore's prosperity is no longer dependent on its role as a place to barter or buy merchandise. It is still a center for the bartering, buying, and transshipment of cargoes, but it is also becoming one of Asia's leading industrial centers. Since 1960, there has been a planned program of industrialization, with light industries at the various estates. The largest industrial estate is at Jurong, operated by the Jurong Town Corporation. It is one of many communities where families live today while the head of the household

THE PORT AND INDUSTRY

works nearby to produce items that range from baked goods and batteries to socks and sugar.

As you enter Jurong, a sign says "Welcome" where a few years ago you could see only barren ground and prawn ponds. Now, you see a sawmill processing giant logs such as Malayan *meranti* to the left of the highway. On the right are blocks of new apartments. Factory buildings make maximum use of land space by being stacked in multistoried "flatted factories." They are making steel pipe and reinforcing bars, plywood and veneer, rubber tires and footwear, pharmaceuticals, and dozens of other products. Workers can pineapples that have been imported from nearby Johore and from Selangor. They splice electric cables, refine sugar, or work in the abattoir or in the pig market. The National Grain Elevator stores flour and animal feed. Workers are busy in the forty-acre fishing port and at Jurong's deepwater wharf. Some are handling bulk cargoes such as cement, coal, and iron ore. Others are employed at the Jurong Shipyard, a joint Singapore government and Japanese business enterprise.

Of course Jurong is not Singapore's only shipyard. The dry docks and other facilities adjoining the Port of Singapore docks, but now operated by a private company, build and repair vessels of all kinds, including patrol boats and small tankers for Ceylon and Malaysia. You can even walk

Along Kim Seng Road, sturdy, blunt-nosed *tongkangs* are produced by Singapore craftsmen who work with small hand tools

THE PORT AND INDUSTRY

along Singapore's Kim Seng Road and find workers hewing beams for traditional Chinese cargo boats, or *tongkangs*. Each boat has two eyes painted on the bow, "so that the ship knows where it is going," or described as "dragon eyes to keep evil away." The workmen use tools that have remained unchanged for generations, although the old *kampong* houses in which they live are rapidly being replaced by tall apartment blocks.

Modern Singapore boat builders are more apt to be found living in a Jurong apartment today, although some still commute from the crowded central city by bus. Those who have moved send their children to the Jurong primary school and enjoy watching their town grow. In their spare time, they can stroll through the town aviary or splash in the Olympic-size swimming pool. In other industrial estates, too, workers engaged in rubber milling, cotton spinning, or motor-vehicle assembly by day enjoy themselves in the markets and theaters of their community by night. This is modern industrial Singapore, where more than two hundred new factories were opened in one eighteen-month period. Here you find that the many cultures of the past and the international trade on which the city was founded have helped to provide the modern Republic with amusements as varied as the origins of the citizens themselves.

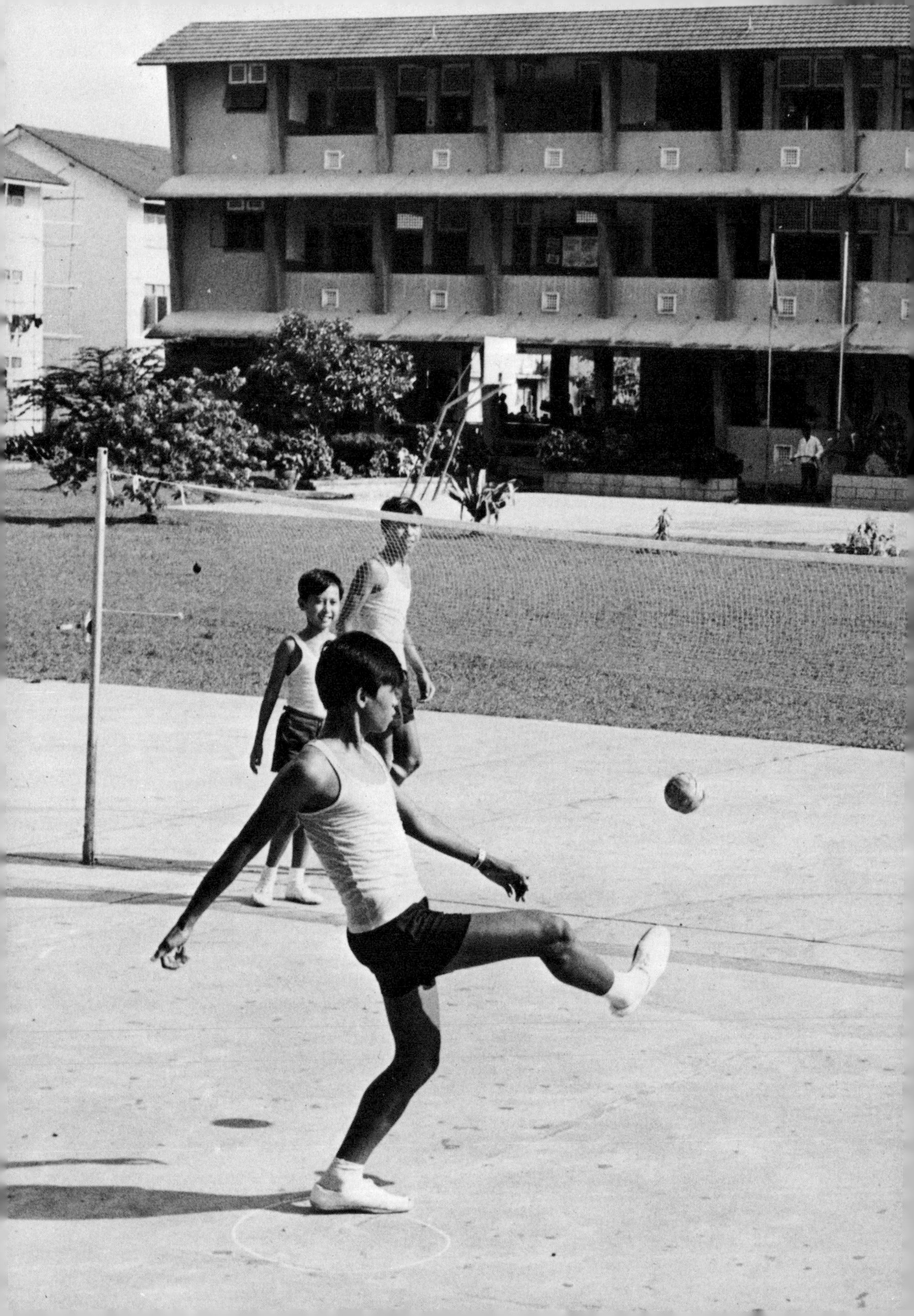

8. At Play in Singapore

ENGLISH cricket and Malay *sepak takraw*, performances of classical Indian dances in Hindu temples or of long-ago Chinese plays at the outdoor *wayang*, American bowling and Japanese judo, table tennis, golf, and polo—all these are waiting for the citizens of Singapore when they finish busy days at the port, in offices, or at school. And like so much of Singapore today, the pastimes have come from past centuries and from countries far away.

Cricket matches are only one example of English influence. Football is usually soccer and not the American game, while Rugby football is a favorite at school. Badminton and hockey are more popular than softball. Primary

Young Singaporeans play the traditional Malay game of *sepak takraw*

students play volleyball, but baseball is virtually unknown. Since the first bowling lanes were opened at the American Club in 1955, however, that game has spread throughout Singapore.

Sepak takraw remains the most popular game not only in primary schools but also for office workers during their lunch hours. This Malay game is more than four hundred years old. It was once played at the court of Alaudin in Malacca. Originally, six or ten players stood in a twenty-foot circle and tried to keep a small ball, weighing six ounces and plaited out of rattan strips, in the air by kicking only. In the modern version, two teams of three stand on either side of a net, using any part of the body except the hands to keep the ball in the air. This is a boys' game, although sometimes the physical-education teacher in primary schools is a woman!

Another favorite sport with boys is *bersilat*, the Malay art of self-defense developed by a fifteenth-century North Sumatran religious teacher at the Malacca court. The unarmed combatant learns to counter any opponent, even one armed with a kris, and sometimes students give *bersilat* performances with a gong-and-drum accompaniment. Judo is the art of Japanese samurai (warriors) of long ago, but today's classes include boys speaking Tamil, Hokkien, English, and Cantonese. Others go to the Chinese YMCA for

A Boy Scout troop assembles for an excursion trip

classes in *taekwando,* the Korean art of self-defense, or in *kung-fu,* Chinese shadowboxing.

    The YMCA and the People's Association are only two of the sponsors of sports and amusements. Extracurricular activities at schools include a dozen different sports, as well as arts and crafts and such groups as the cadets. Seventeen thousand uniformed cadets—air, army, police, and sea—drill on Saturday mornings. The familiar uniforms of Boy Scouts and Girl Scouts are on the scene too, although the girls use the English name, "Girl Guides." Red Cross and St. John's Ambulance Brigade classes provide practical training and give students the opportunity to help others.

    These international programs contrast with programs of ancient arts and music. You might hear a bugle-and-fife band in a primary school, or join one of Singapore's fifty-six brass bands. There is even a band where the only instrument is the harmonica! But you can also hear the sounds of

LIVING IN SINGAPORE

Chinese cymbals and of the Indian *nagaswaram* (windpipe). Few students, however, will have an opportunity to play the *gendang* ("big drum"), *nafari* (a kind of trumpet), and other instruments of the Malay court.

At the annual Youth Festival, students share Singapore's multiracial heritage of songs, music, and dancing. A group of Chinese girls may perform a Scottish dance accompanied by a bagpipe band. Malay girls practice the movements of the Chinese tea pickers' and umbrella dances. Indian girls learn the Malay *tarian tempurong*, celebrating the coconut harvest, using half-shells of coconuts to keep time. Boys perform the exciting Dragon Dance or Lion

Singapore students perform a Chinese dance at the Youth Festival

AT PLAY IN SINGAPORE

Dance of ancient China, while girls of Malay, Chinese, Indian, and European ancestry join in the Javanese Candle Dance.

Students also take pride in performing the dances of their own particular heritage. Chinese girls gracefully dance the Rolling Lantern or the classic Song of the Rainbow Skirts. Indian girls may perform dances traditionally associated with worship at Hindu temples. Each gesture of these dances has a special meaning. The hand may be held so that the fingers curve to suggest an open lotus blossom. According to the position in which the hand is held, this gesture may represent the full moon or a mirror or even a bird. Two hands held to the head in this gesture may symbolize a mountain. In some dances, the performers wear anklets of tiny bells, or tall crowns, or jeweled costumes and elaborate makeup.

Enjoyment of traditional dances is not confined to schoolchildren. Families enjoy weekend and evening concerts that include government-sponsored performances designed to keep the ancient dances and music alive. Singaporeans all enjoy the Malay *ronggeng*, too, for it is no longer confined to the *kampongs*. Musicians play while members of the audience come to join the girls on stage: but the partners in this dance must never touch! You can also relive the past at the National Museum, where the arts of the

Malays are shown. These include the traditional puppets of the *wayang kulit*. The puppets are made of buffalo hide with bamboo struts, and the puppeteer can manipulate two at a time so that their shadows are cast on the curtain between the puppeteer and his audience.

This Malay shadow play can also be seen at Singapore's Gay World, Great World, and New World. These Chinese amusement centers are favorite places for a family outing, even though they do not really come alive until late in the evening. Most of the families are Chinese, but as the lights come on and people arrive, you notice an occasional Sikh turban, and Malay and English voices mingle with the Chinese dialects.

At the Great World in Kim Seng Road, you can go shopping for clothes or for uniquely Chinese foods, or pause for a bowl of noodles and a piece of watermelon. Things for sale include giant goldfish with bulging eyes, gaily singing birds, and miniature trees a hundred years old. A group of old men are drinking cups of pale Chinese tea, while children nearby ride a small merry-go-round. Children even have their own billiard room, where they enjoy a game that was played at Singapore's first billiard club back in 1829.

If you miss the performance of Malay puppets, you may still find a Chinese puppet show. There are Hokkien glove puppets accompanied by backstage musicians, and Hokchew string puppets. Dance programs range from a Chinese handkerchief dance to Malay *joget*. You can always count on seeing a good movie, including Cinerama, and there is *wayang* on an open-air stage.

The *wayang* often seems the entertainment most characteristic of Singapore, especially of its Chinese residents. As you walk through the streets of Chinatown, you will see workmen erecting the temporary stage and its bamboo framework. A festival, an anniversary, or a neighborhood party—all are occasions for hiring a *wayang* troupe. The backstage area is open for all the passersby to see. Children climb on stage, grandmothers hold babies and squat on cartons outside the shop-houses, and girls and boys on their way home from school pause to listen to the high-pitched voices of the gaily costumed players. Stories of long-ago princesses, emperors, and magic are reenacted on the stage to the clashing accompaniment of cymbals and gongs.

At Tiger Balm Garden there is another kind of Chinese entertainment. Here the brothers Aw Boon Haw and Aw Boon Par built a unique display of fantastic statues. The hillside is covered with figures from Chinese legends. Grottoes and caves include realistic tableaux of the tortures of the Chinese Hell. Not all the figures are Chinese, however. The painted concrete statues include two outsize figures of Japanese *sumo* (traditional wrestling) champions, along with an advertisement for the brothers' Tiger Balm Oil.

At Tiger Balm Garden, figures of Japanese *sumo* wrestlers show off their concrete strength

There are even Walt Disney cartoon characters.

These are unique Singapore pastimes, but others are like those enjoyed in the United States. Picnics and a day at the beach are especially popular. No one lives more than seven miles from the coast, and the island of Singapore has its own cluster of small offshore islands as well. Every weekend, families journey by bus and car to the beach at Changi, where they lie in the sand, swim, or camp in "caravans" (the English word for house trailer). Refreshments at the beach include everything from Malay *satay* to English fish and chips.

Other beaches are noted for underwater swimming. At Mersing, off the coast of Johore, for instance, Singapore

AT PLAY IN SINGAPORE

boys can put on goggles or use a glass-bottomed bucket to watch tropical fish in the clear water. They can explore coral gardens, too, although they have to watch out for barracuda and shark. Of course, they can also look at tropical fish right in Singapore, at the Van Kleef Aquarium, especially when the heavy monsoon rains of November to March cloud the ocean water.

Some excursions require a journey by one of the small boats for hire at Clifford Pier, although to go fishing you need to travel only a few miles by car to Singapore's freshwater ponds, where a two-dollar fee permits you to keep any fish under three pounds. A half-hour bus ride takes you into the jungle. Giant trees more than 150 feet high, thick creepers, and tropical plants have been preserved in the Bukit Timah Nature Reserve. A few mangrove swamps remain at Pandan, and occasionally visitors can see an ar-

Malay teen-agers and a European family spend Sunday at the beach

cherfish like the one on Singapore's six-cent stamp. This fish uses a jet of water to knock ants from leaves and above the water.

Singapore does have its share of wild and even dangerous animals, but you are unlikely to encounter the poisonous snakes such as king and black cobras. There are more than thirty kinds of snakes on the island altogether, however, and you can find several varieties suitable for keeping as pets. It is still possible to catch a glimpse of the flying lemur, the scaly anteater, and the green heron, but as Singapore's industries and housing developments spread into former mangrove swamps and forest areas, such sights become increasingly rare.

Some wild monkeys, though, are right in the city, at the Botanic Gardens. These small monkeys (long-tailed macaques) provide Singapore families with much amusement, especially the mothers that scamper around with baby monkeys clinging frantically to their fur. In these gardens, where Malaya's first rubber was grown, you can wander through a tiny patch of carefully preserved jungle, or watch black Australian swans gliding across the lake. No one is permitted to pick the hundreds of orchids on display. But eight hundred varieties of orchids grow on the Malay Peninsula, and many of the varieties grown in Singapore's famous nurseries are for sale in the markets of the city.

At Singapore's Botanic Gardens, a mother and her children take a close-up view of another mother and child

Markets, magazines, exhibits, and shows are all part of a day's fun in Singapore. The magazines include stories about Indian and Malay film stars, photos of "clothes for swingers," and requests for pen pals. There are "things-to-swap" columns, where one student wants to exchange his guitar course for a tape recorder and books. "Man in Space" is a modern exhibit, but a demonstration of ancient Korean pottery-making techniques can be seen a few blocks away. Once a month, there is another colorful sight:

109

Two Indian girls watch a Tamil movie on Singapore TV. They can also read the English subtitles, since that is their second language at school

the Changing of the Guard at the Istana Negara, where soldiers guarding the President's Palace march back and forth. They stamp their feet rhythmically while the band plays exciting tunes.

Stay-at-homes can enjoy TV in Singapore just as they can in the United States, but there is one big difference. Many of the programs have subtitles in a second language (for instance, Malay or English subtitles on Chinese films). A typical day's programs include *Run for Your Life* in Cantonese; a Malay feature film, *Anak Laut*; Part Three of a Teochew opera, *Four Appeals*; world-famous stories in Tamil; and an English serial! Another day brings *Madam White Snake* in Cantonese, programs of Malay music, Skippy the Bush Kangaroo, and an adventure series filmed in Australia. Cantonese feature films, Oriental art, career ideas, and the latest from Hollywood alternate with the Tamil version of Aladdin.

Singapore offers entertainments from A to Z, in fact, beginning with Archery, Badminton, and Cricket, and ending with Yachting and *Zapin*. *Zapin* is a combination of Arabic and Malay music and dancing, with male performers, which came from the courts of Arabia in the fifteenth century. Such links with the past are a familiar part of life in Singapore, especially during the many festivals celebrated in the modern city.

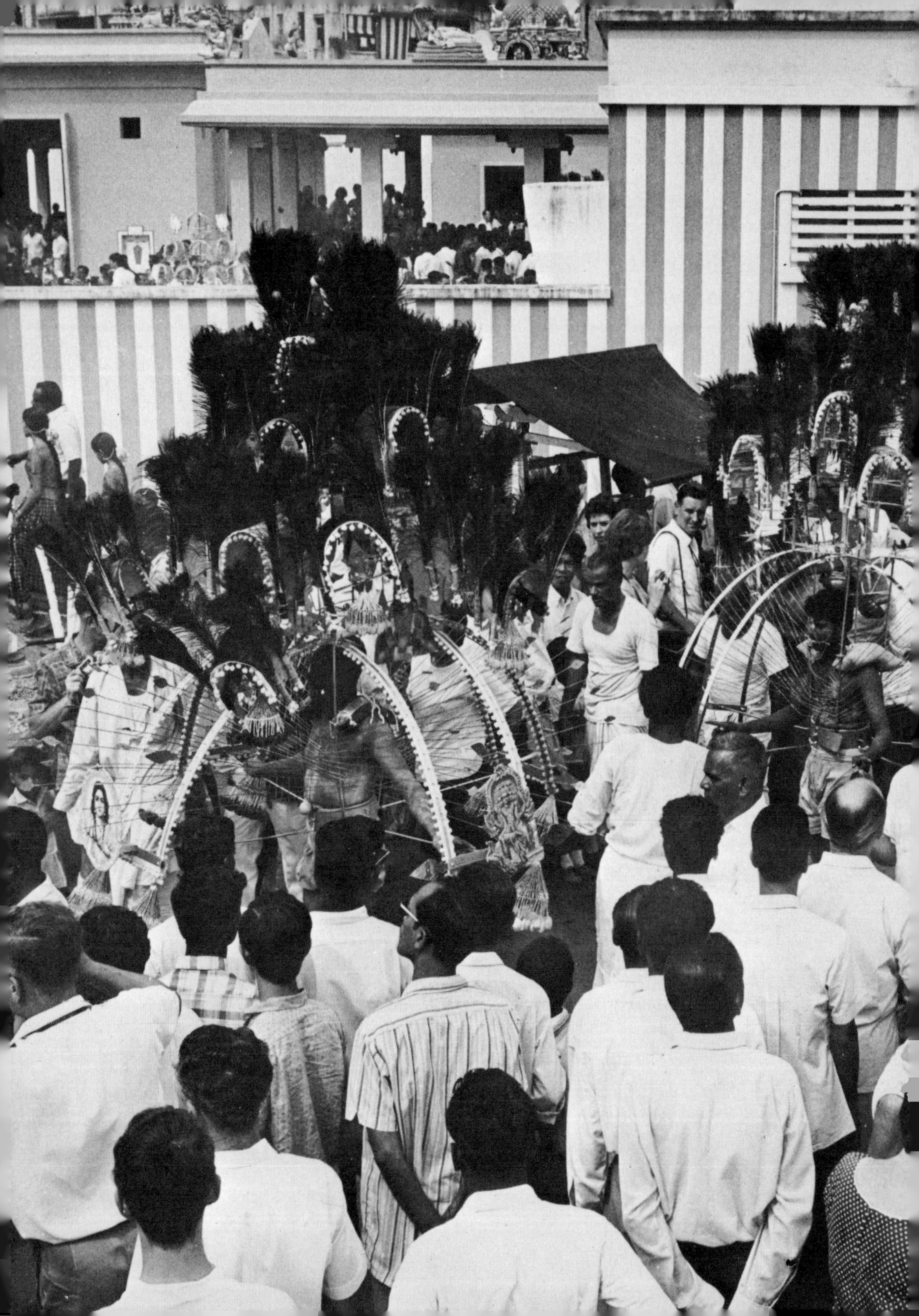

9. Festivals and Celebrations

SINGAPORE'S calendar includes dozens of holidays, feast days, and anniversaries. The multiracial and religious groups who have contributed their special days to the Singapore calendar are many: Chinese, Malay, Tamil, Hindu, Moslem, Taoist, Sikh, Christian, Jewish, Punjabi, Malayalee, Singhalese (from Ceylon), and more. Some of these days are official holidays for everyone in the Republic, including both the Western New Year's Day and two days for the Chinese New Year. Other national holidays are the Moslem Hari Raya Puasa and Hari Raya Haji, the Hindu Deepavali, the birthdays of Buddha and of Christ, the

---

In the Hindu festival Thaipusam, devotees carry *kavadis* through the streets. Month-long fasting and preparation enable them to endure the multiple punctures from steel darts suspended from the frames

LIVING IN SINGAPORE

Christian Good Friday, Labor Day (May 1), and National Day (August 9).

New Year celebrations in Singapore are not confined to the two holidays on the official calendar, however. In April, there is a Hindu New Year, for those whose ancestors were Tamils, Malayalee, or Singhalese. This date in April is known as Baisakhi to the Sikhs. It is their New Year and also the birthday of the Sikh religion (founded by Nanak in the fifteenth century). Singapore's Jewish community celebrates Rosh Hashanah in the fall. Jewish children also observe Tu-B'Shvat, New Year for Trees, planting trees as they do in Israel, in January or February, according to the Jewish calendar.

The Moslem year begins with Muharram (first month), although there is no celebration. Instead, accounts are settled and visits exchanged at Hari Raya Puasa. The exact date of this holiday depends on the time at which holy men sight the new moon. On this most sacred day for Moslems, men go to pray at the mosque immediately after morning bathing. Families dress in new clothes and entertain with sweetmeats and specially prepared foods as they visit one another during the first two days, while they often enjoy some sort of public entertainment on the third.

Hari Raya Puasa celebrates the end of Ramadan, the month in which the Koran was sent down. The Koran was

FESTIVALS AND CELEBRATIONS

given on the twentieth day of this month, and today mosques and homes are specially illuminated for the occasion. Ramadan is the time when all true Moslems fast from dawn to dusk. Of course, they do not go without food entirely. Each day during Ramadan they eat a big meal at ten o'clock at night, and then get up for an early meal before dawn.

Hari Raya Haji falls on the tenth day of the twelfth month of the Moslem calendar. Pilgrims were supposed to reach Mecca on this day. Men who have completed the pilgrimage attend special services at the mosque. It is also the custom to give alms.

Most Malay festivals are related to the Moslem calendar, although the celebration of Mandi Safar at Changi beaches includes dancing and picnics as well as the religious cleansing. Chinese festivals also can be linked with religious beliefs. Some are associated with Taoist belief, while a few are Buddhist, and Confucius is honored too.

Chinese festivals, like the New Year, are celebrated according to the lunar calendar, in which the first month falls between mid-January and mid-February according to Western dates. Streets are noisy with the sound of exploding firecrackers at the New Year and the sidewalks turn red as explosions throw off the firecrackers' red-paper covering. The New Year is really a family festival rather than a

Singapore Chinese burn joss sticks and candles during the Festival of the Nine Emperor Gods

public one, however. Housewives stock up on special foods, especially large quantities of oranges. The color of oranges suggests gold and hence a prosperous year. Children are given packets of lucky money, *ang pow*. The money is usually new Singapore dollar bills or shiny new coins placed in a red-and-gold envelope. Special Straits Chinese foods are served, and families enjoy excursions. In the warm tropical afternoon, hundreds throng Tiger Balm Garden and other amusement centers.

Two other Chinese festivals bring enjoyment to many

FESTIVALS AND CELEBRATIONS

residents of Singapore: the Moon Festival and the Festival of the Nine Emperor Gods, both celebrated during autumn. The Chinese do not see the Western "Man in the Moon" but a Hare or Rabbit. On the fifteenth day of the eighth moon, they remember the legend of the Hare who gave his life for Buddha. The Hare, Fox, and Monkey were practicing Bodhisattva discipline. Buddha came disguised as a hungry old man to test them, but the Hare could find nothing to match the offerings of the others. So he decided to roast himself. He flung himself on the enchanted charcoal of Buddha's fire; Buddha resumed his own shape, and then sent the Hare to the moon. A cloud wisp is said to be smoke from the roasting Hare.

The streets of Chinatown are gay with enormous decorated candles, pictures of the Moon Goddess, and of the Hare, whose portrait is later burned so that he can return to the moon. Children carry lanterns in the form of rabbits, fish, or butterflies, and there are temporary altars in the streets, with elaborately decorated candles. But it is the moon cake that best symbolizes the occasion. This is a shell of heavy pastry enclosing a mixture of sweet beans, duck egg, ground nuts, spices, and lotus seeds, often with meat and other ingredients as well. The Chinese ideogram for "moon" or a picture of the "Hare in the Moon" is stamped on the top of the cake. Offerings of moon cakes, as well as

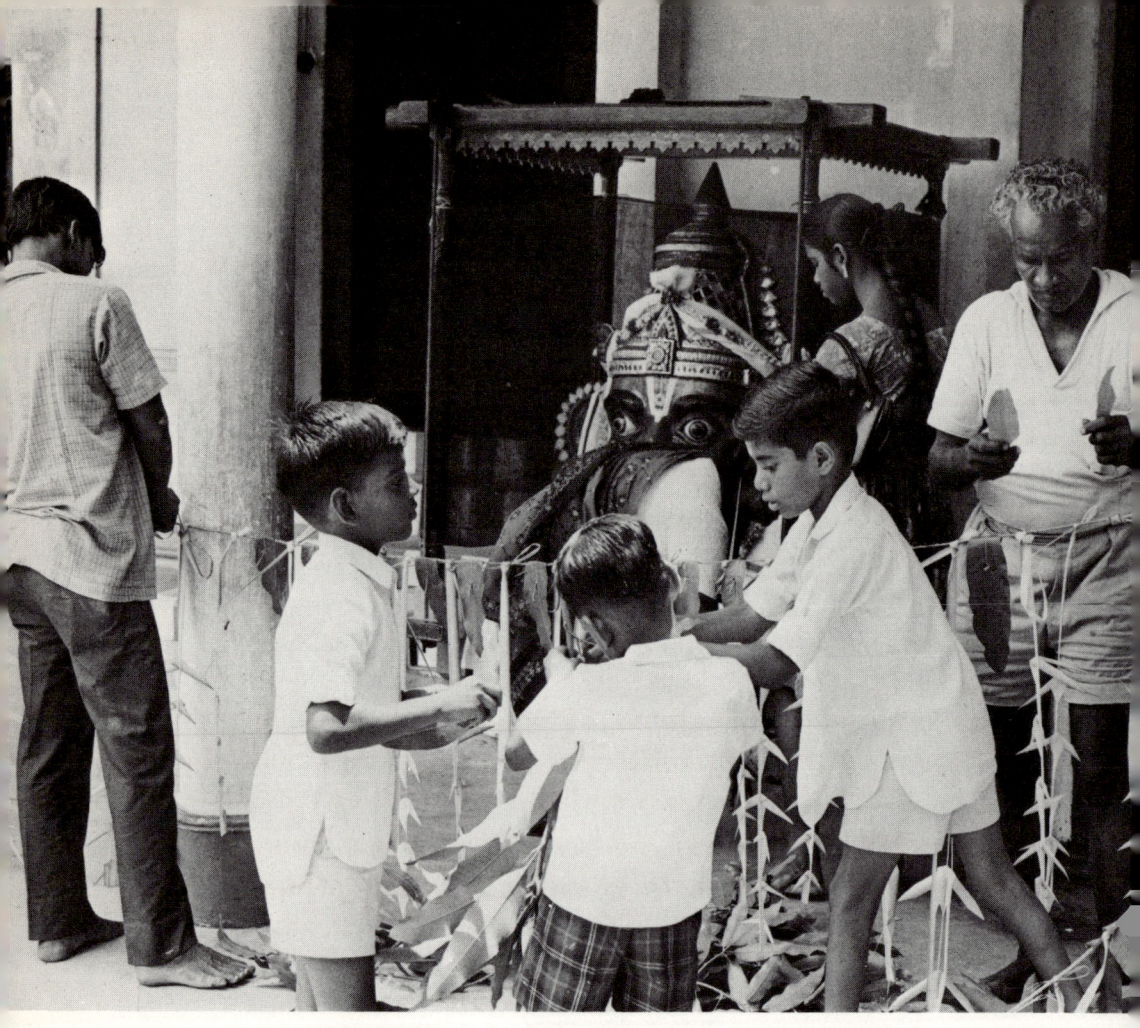

Hindu boys help make decorations for a religious celebration

five dishes of fruits, are placed on family altars. Joss sticks are burned, too, and people burn paper clothes as offerings for the Moon Goddess.

During the days of the Moon Festival, you see the *way-ang* set up in the streets of Singapore. On the Festival of

FESTIVALS AND CELEBRATIONS

the Nine Emperor Gods, beginning on the first day of the ninth moon, you will see performers using the permanent *wayang* stage at the temple dedicated to the Goddess of the North Pole Star. This festival continues for nine days, with the return of the gods celebrated on the ninth day, and you can see families burning joss sticks, making offerings, and enjoying picnics and entertainments at the temple.

The Indians and Pakistanis have their colorful celebrations, too. Moslem Indians celebrate the same days as the Malay Moslems, of course, but the Hindus have festivals of their own. Deepavali is the Hindu festival of lights. As on Chinese New Year, merchants settle accounts and may redecorate shops and offices. The holiday resembles Christmas in being a time for the exchange of gifts. Greeting cards are exchanged, too, resembling the familiar New Year and Christmas cards of other countries, but with pictures of the elephant-headed Ganesha, of Krishna playing his flute, and of Vishnu and his consort Lakshmi. Families make their homes gay with candles and *dipa* (oil lamps) and hang lamps on poles at the door, while children light sparklers. For Lakshmi, Goddess of Wealth, will not visit dark places.

There are several versions of the legend in different parts of India, but the festival celebrates Lord Krishna's killing

A vendor displays greeting cards for the Hindu festival of Deepavali

of the tyrant king Narakasura. It is said that Narakasura came from his fortress in the Himalayas to trouble the gods. The *devas* (minor gods) asked Vishnu for help. Vishnu, in his incarnation as Krishna, then fought and slew Narakasura.

In contrast to the family celebration of Deepavali, the festival of Thaipusam moves through the streets of Singapore. A pair of white oxen pull the silver chariot of Lord Subramania through the streets, surrounded by devotees.

FESTIVALS AND CELEBRATIONS

Lord Subramania has thirty-seven names. He has six heads and twelve arms to symbolize his various divine qualities. Legend says that he used the peacock as a chariot, and peacock feathers are used during this festival as well as being placed on the family altar throughout the year. Before the procession begins, you can see worshipers breaking coconut shells before the image of Lord Subramania, to indicate prayers answered or wishes fulfilled. As on other special occasions, the air is fragrant with burning sandalwood and flower petals scattered on the altars.

The most unusual part of this festival is the carrying of

A Hindu worshiper, garlanded with flowers and carrying a pot of honey on his head, watches preparations for the Thaipusam procession *kavadis* by devout men. For the month preceding the festival, they eat only one meal a day. Then they fast for twenty-four hours. At the Hindu temple on Serangoon Road, silver and steel darts or needles are thrust through their tongues and cheeks or into their bodies. Some of these spikes have weights on one end, or containers of milk. The *kavadi*, a great semicircular steel frame, is held on the shoulders by supporting bars and covered with peacock feathers and flowers. Although there may be several dozen of these spikes on a single *kavadi*, no blood is drawn, and the men feel no pain. They carry their *kavadis* in procession through the streets, and at the end of the festival, which includes dancing, the steel is removed from the men's bodies.

These are only a few of the festive occasions in Singapore. The ways in which holidays are celebrated are as varied as their origins. Sikhs always celebrate at their temples, as on the birthday of their religion's fifteenth-century founder, Nanak. Firecrackers mark many Chinese festivals, but those who are Buddhist also share in quiet meditation, as on Vesak, the celebration of the birthday of Buddha in 523 B.C. and his subsequent enlightenment and death. They meditate on the ten precepts of Buddhism and display six-color flags, the colors of the rays of Lord Buddha's halo. Buddhist bird-liberation days, Christmas carols at St.

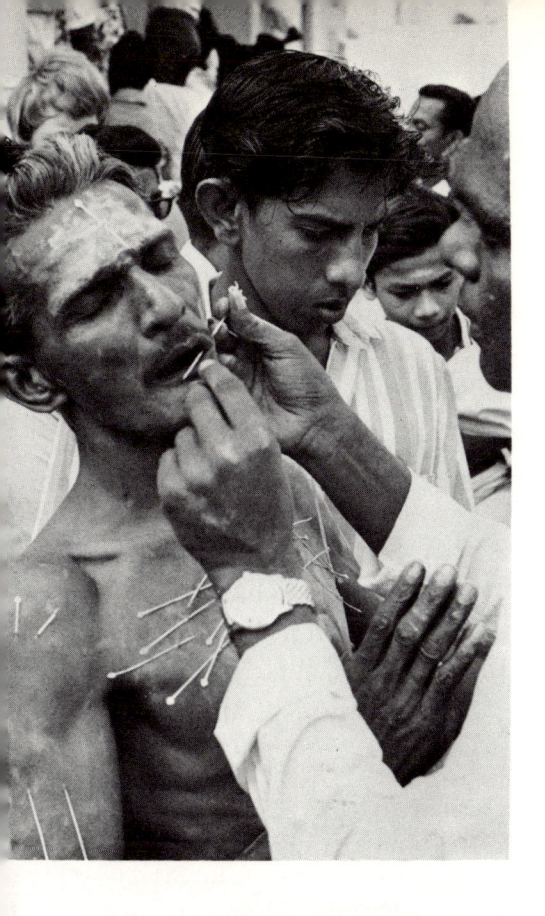

As a devotee is prepared for the Thaipusam procession, silver darts or needles are inserted in his body. They pierce his lips, tongue, and forehead, but no blood is drawn.

Andrew's Cathedral, Jewish parties at Hanukkah and Purim—all are part of the year's religious ceremonies. There are Taoist pilgrimages to Kusu Island to pray to the God of Prosperity, and several festivals honoring Kuan Yin, Buddhist Goddess of Mercy. The Malayalees celebrate a day on which the spirit of a long-ago king visits them.

One of the most solemn birthdays includes no parties, although there are feasts for the poor, and Moslem youths gather to compete in readings of the Koran. That day is

LIVING IN SINGAPORE

Mohammed's birthday, marked with religious processions and prayers. But there is another birthday that includes marching bands, parades of military and civil organizations, and a grand illumination and decoration of public buildings. That is August 9, National Day, celebrating the birth of the Republic in 1965.

On this day, Singaporeans may look back to long-ago Malay rulers, Chinese planters, Indian merchants, Arab traders, and seafarers of many nations. They think of the Sea Town, Temasek, and of the naming of their city Singapura. But they also think about the future of their Lion

Singapore has four official languages: Malay, Chinese, Tamil, and English. These government offices display all four.

FESTIVALS AND CELEBRATIONS

City. The Youth Festival, with its exhibitions of thousand-year-old dances, present-day youth groups, and songs of the future, reminds everyone that Singapore is a young city and a republic, too. The teen-agers who sing and dance in the tradition of their multiracial heritage, and who are among Singapore's under-twenty population majority, also remind you why it is so exciting to be living in Singapore. This is the newest, busiest, and most enterprising city in Asia today. People of many cultures, speaking many languages, and worshiping many gods all live together in harmony, and plan for their future as citizens of Singapore.

Majulah Singapura! (Progress Singapore!)

Index

Agriculture, 11, 32, 34, 87-88. See also Crops
Airport, 93
America, Americans, 11, 13, 26, 39, 72, 86, 90, 99, 100
Amusements, 20, 97, 104-107
Apartments, 19, 20-26, 29, 32, 35-36, 43
Arabs, 46, 111
Arts and Crafts, 42-43, 52-53, 91, 103-104

Batik, 52-53
Bazaars, 14-15
Boatbuilding. See Shipbuilding
Boats. See Ships
Botanic Gardens, 89, 108-109
Brahma, 63
Buddha, Buddhists, 15, 42, 63, 70-71, 113, 115, 117, 122-123

Calendar, 113-115
China, Chinese, 9-15, 19, 24-26, 30-43, 46, 55, 75, 78, 79, 80, 84, 90, 94, 102-105, 111, 115-119, 122. See also Straits Chinese
Christ, Christians, 15, 20, 60, 63-64, 66, 113-115
Christmas, 113, 122
Clan associations, 42-43
Climate and weather, 22, 84-85, 107, 116
Clothes and fashions, 9-10, 19, 34-35, 51-53, 57, 58-63, 68, 109
Confucius, 115
Cooking, 17, 24-27, 53-55, 66-67, 69. See Spices.
Craftsmen, 33, 40, 42-43, 52-53, 96-97
Cricket, 83, 99
Crops, 32, 34, 38, 53-54, 87-89. See also Rubber; Spices

Customs and traditions, 19, 34, 40-43, 46-47, 49-50, 57, 63-64, 68-69, 74. See also Festivals

Dancing, 60, 99, 102-105, 111, 115, 122
Deepavali, 113, 119-120
Department stores, 14
Dragon Teeth Gate, 9, 12

East India Company, 11, 16, 33, 58, 84
Eating stalls. See Restaurants
Education. See Schools; Universities
English, 11, 29, 46, 60, 66, 74, 84, 89, 99, 106. See also Language
Estates, 20-21, 97. See also Jurong, Queenstown
Europe, Europeans, 11-12, 14-15, 26, 39, 58, 66, 88, 92-93

Festivals, 112-113, 115-122
Food, 17, 19, 24-29, 34, 36-40, 45, 50, 53-55, 60-61, 64, 66-68, 73-74, 104, 106, 114, 115-117
Football, 60, 99

Gardens and parks, 22-23, 89, 108. See also Tiger Balm Garden; Wildlife.
Geography, 10-11, 15-16, 84-86
Government, 16

Hari Raya Haji, 113, 115
Hari Raya Puasa, 113-115
Health and hygiene, 16-17, 40-41, 43, 83
Hindus, 14, 31, 35, 57, 58, 63-68, 103, 112-113, 118-123
History, 11-13, 16, 32-33, 45, 57-58, 84-85
Holidays, 113-114, 122. See also Fes-

126

tivals and individual celebrations
Homes and furnishings, 19-29, 32, 35-36, 43, 47-49, 54, 63-64, 68-69

Ideograms, *See* Writing
Inche Yusof bin Ishak. *See* Yusof
India, Indians, 9-11, 15, 26, 35, 55, 56-69, 84, 102-103, 109, 113, 119. *See also* Hindus, Moslems, Pakistanis, Sikhs
Indonesia, 9, 11, 13, 15, 45-46, 83, 85-87, 89-90, 93
Industry, 77, 79, 81, 86, 90, 92-95, 97. *See also* Jurong
Islam. *See* Moslems
Istana Negara, 111

Johore, 95
Johore, Sultan of, 11, 33, 84
Joss sticks, 90, 116, 118-119
Jungle, 107-108
Jurong, 21-22, 92, 94-95, 97

Kampong, 19, 47-49, 69, 103. *See also* Malays
Kelong, 48-49
Koran, 46, 72, 114-115, 123

Language, 9-11, 16, 26, 34-35, 42, 45-46, 57, 63, 69, 71-75, 78-81, 100, 110-111, 124. *See also* Writing
Lao Tzu. *See* Taoists
Lee Kuan Yew, 16, 32
Legends, 105, 117, 119-121
Lion City, 9, 12

Magazines and newspapers, 91, 109
Malacca, 57-58, 100
Malay Annals, 12

Malay Peninsula, 11, 15, 45, 57, 84-85, 89, 91, 106-108
Malays, 9-11, 15, 26, 33-34, 44-55, 57, 61, 69, 71-72, 75-76, 83, 99-100, 102-105, 107, 111, 113, 115, 119
Malaysia, 16, 33, 86, 90, 95
Markets, 14-15, 21, 25-26, 38, 45
Mecca, 62, 115
Minerals and gems, 11-12, 14, 86, 91. *See also* Oil, mineral; Tin
Mohammed, 50, 124
Moon Festival, 117-118
Moslems, 35, 46-47, 50-53, 62, 71-72, 113-115, 119, 123-124
Movies, 105, 111
Music, 9, 65-66, 78, 101-103, 105, 111

Names, 46, 61
National Day, 114, 124
National holidays, 113-114
National language, 11, 75
New Year celebrations, 113-116
Nine Emperor Gods, 116-117, 119

Occupations, 11, 14, 17, 21-22, 31-34, 36-37, 40-43, 46, 49-50, 58, 61-63, 79-81, 83, 87, 91, 93, 95-97, 105
Oil, mineral, 13, 86, 91-94
vegetable, 86, 89-91

Pakistanis, 15, 58, 60, 63, 66, 119
Population, 9-10, 15, 31-32, 45, 58
Port, 11-13, 83-94, 95
Pulau Brani, 47-48, 90
Pulau Bukom, 92-94

Queenstown, 20, 21, 23-25, 29

127

Radio and Television, 34-35, 69, 110-111
Raffles, Sir Stamford, 11, 32, 45, 47, 81, 84, 88, 90
Ramadan, 114-115
Religion, 14-15, 20, 35, 46-47, 50-51, 53, 57, 60, 62-66, 72, 90, 112-124
Restaurants, 17, 36-37, 39-40, 67-68, 104
Rubber, 12, 58, 86, 88-90, 108

Sang Nila Utama, 12
Schools, 20-21, 28-29, 50, 51, 60, 69, 70-81
Sea people, 47
Sea Town. *See* Temasek
Self-defense, arts of, 79, 100-101
Sepak takraw, 83, 98-100
Shipbuilding and boatbuilding, 95-97
Ships and boats, 12, 13, 84, 86-88, 93, 94, 95-97
Shop-houses, 19, 36
Shops, 10, 14, 20, 36, 40-41. *See also* Bazaars; Markets
Sikhs, 59, 60, 61-62, 68, 75, 76, 114, 122
Singapore River, 9, 87
Spices, 11, 12, 36-38, 53, 66-67, 86, 88

Sports and games, 60, 77-79, 83, 97, 99-101, 104, 111
Straits Chinese, 34, 37, 49, 55, 116
Suez Canal, 13, 92
Supermarkets, 14, 25-26, 39

Tamil, 10, 57, 63, 69, 71, 74-75, 81, 110-111
Taoists, 15, 70-71, 113, 115, 123
Temasek, 12, 32, 57-58
Temples, 14, 15, 20, 31, 32, 35, 64-65, 67, 90, 103, 119, 122
Thaipusam, 112-113, 120-123
Theaters, plays, and puppets, 6, 79, 99, 104, 105, 118-119
Tiger Balm Garden, 105-106, 116
Tin, 12, 34, 58, 89-91
Tongkang, 13, 86-87, 96-97
Trade, 11-13, 57, 83-86, 88-95
Transportation, 10, 13, 29, 34, 89, 107. *See also* Ships and boats

Universities, 80

Vesak Day, 122

Wildlife, 22-23, 72, 107-109
Writing, 10, 41-42, 71, 117

Youth Festival, 79, 102, 125
Youth organizations, 100-101, 125
Yusof bin Ishak, Inche, 16, 46

915.95
Boa Boardman

AUTHOR

Living in Singapore

TITLE

DATE DUE

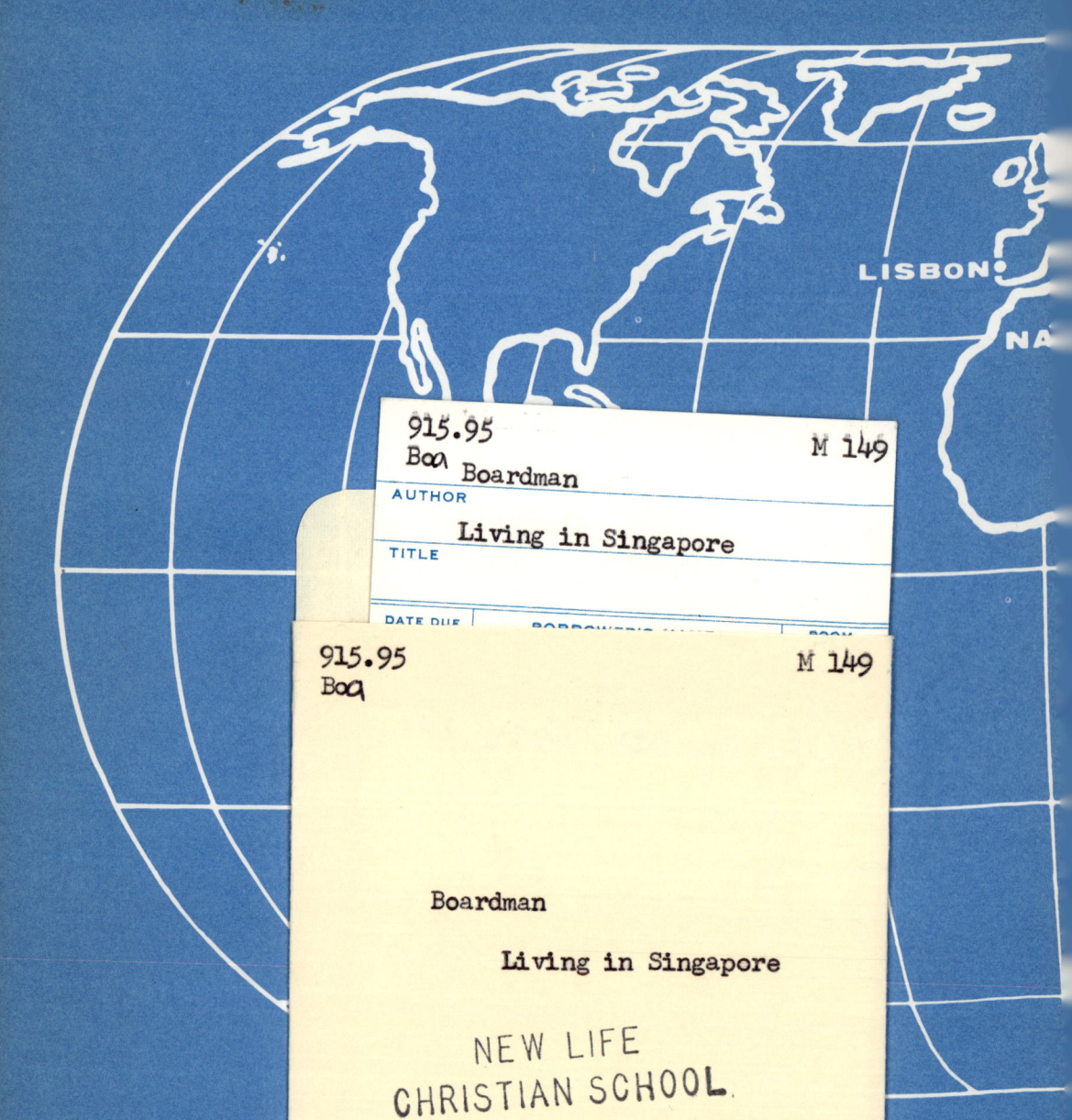

915.95   M 149
Boa

Boardman

Living in Singapore

NEW LIFE
CHRISTIAN SCHOOL.

North St. Paul - Maplewood Schools
Maplewood Jr. High Library